W9-BMR-724

Great-Tasting Potatoes

Publications International, Ltd.

Copyright © 2010 Publications International, Ltd.
All rights reserved. This publication may not be reproduced or quoted in whole or in part by any means whatsoever without written permission from:

Louis Weber, CEO
Publications International, Ltd.
7373 North Cicero Avenue
Lincolnwood, IL 60712

Permission is never granted for commercial purposes.

Favorite Brand Name Recipes is a trademark of Publications International, Ltd.

All recipes and photographs that contain specific brand names are copyrighted by those companies and/or associations, unless otherwise specified. All photographs *except* those on pages 9, 13, 19, 73, 87 and 113 copyright © Publications International, Ltd.

Campbell's® and Swanson® registered trademarks of CSC Brands LP. All rights reserved.

Carnation is a registered trademark of Nestlé.

Some of the products listed in this publication may be in limited distribution.

Pictured on the front cover: Roasted Peppers and Potatoes *(page 84)*.
Pictured on the back cover *(top to bottom):* Spicy African Chickpea and Sweet Potato Stew *(page 60)* and Taco-Topped Potatoes *(page 98)*.

ISBN-13: 978-1-60553-707-8
ISBN-10: 1-60553-707-1

Library of Congress Control Number: 2010922436

Manufactured in China.

8 7 6 5 4 3 2 1

Microwave Cooking: Microwave ovens vary in wattage. Use the cooking times as guidelines and check for doneness before adding more time.

Preparation/Cooking Times: Preparation times are based on the approximate amount of time required to assemble the recipe before cooking, baking, chilling or serving. These times include preparation steps such as measuring, chopping and mixing. The fact that some preparations and cooking can be done simultaneously is taken into account. Preparation of optional ingredients and serving suggestions is not included.

Publications International, Ltd.

table of contents

spud soups & chowders 4

meat & potato meals 26

international taters 48

mashed, fried & on the side 72

stuffed, baked & roasted 94

salads, snacks & more 116

acknowledgments 139

index 140

potato cheddar soup

2 pounds new red potatoes, cut into ½-inch cubes
¾ cup coarsely chopped carrots
1 medium onion, coarsely chopped
3 cups chicken broth
½ teaspoon salt
1 cup half-and-half
¼ teaspoon black pepper
2 cups (8 ounces) shredded Cheddar cheese

Slow Cooker Directions

1. Layer potatoes, carrots, onion, broth and salt in slow cooker. Cover; cook on LOW 6 to 7 hours or on HIGH 3 to 3½ hours or until vegetables are tender.

2. Stir in half-and-half and pepper. Cover; cook on HIGH 15 minutes. Turn off heat. Let stand, uncovered, 5 minutes. Stir in cheese until melted.

Makes 6 servings

spud soups & chowders

hearty vegetable stew

1 tablespoon olive oil
1 cup chopped onion
¾ cup chopped carrots
3 cloves garlic, minced
4 cups coarsely chopped green cabbage
3½ cups coarsely chopped unpeeled new red potatoes
1 teaspoon salt
1 teaspoon dried rosemary
½ teaspoon black pepper
4 cups vegetable broth
1 can (about 15 ounces) Great Northern beans, rinsed and drained
1 can (about 14 ounces) diced tomatoes

1. Heat oil in large saucepan over medium-high heat. Add onion and carrots; cook and stir 3 minutes. Add garlic; cook and stir 1 minute.

2. Add cabbage, potatoes, salt, rosemary and pepper; cook 1 minute. Stir in broth, beans and tomatoes; bring to a boil. Reduce heat to low; simmer 15 minutes or until potatoes are tender. **Makes 6 servings**

rustic vegetable soup

1 to 2 baking potatoes, cut into ½-inch pieces
1 package (10 ounces) frozen mixed vegetables, thawed
1 package (10 ounces) frozen cut green beans, thawed
1 green bell pepper, chopped
1 jar (16 ounces) picante sauce
1 can (about 10 ounces) condensed beef broth, undiluted
¼ cup finely chopped fresh parsley

Slow Cooker Directions

Combine all ingredients except parsley in slow cooker. Cover; cook on LOW 8 hours or on HIGH 4 hours. Stir in parsley. **Makes 8 servings**

hearty vegetable stew

curried carrot and potato soup

1 medium DOLE® Onion, chopped
2 cloves garlic, minced
1 tablespoon olive oil
1 teaspoon curry powder
4 cups reduced sodium, fat-free chicken broth
1 package (16 ounces) DOLE® Mini Cut Carrots
1 large DOLE® Russet Potato (about 12 ounces), peeled and cubed
⅛ teaspoon white pepper
1 to 1½ cups milk
Chopped chives or parsley (optional)

• Sauté onion and garlic in oil in large saucepot, over medium-high heat, stirring frequently, about 5 minutes. Add curry powder; cook, stirring 1 to 2 minutes longer.

• Add broth, carrots, potato and pepper; bring to boil. Reduce heat; simmer, covered, until vegetables are very tender, about 10 to 15 minutes. Cool slightly. Purée in batches in covered blender or food processor container.

• Return soup to saucepot. Stir in milk; heat, stirring occasionally. Do not boil. Garnish with chives or parsley, if desired. **Makes 8 servings**

Prep Time: 34 minutes

curried carrot and potato soup

cream-cheesy garden chowder

1 can (about 14 ounces) chicken broth
2 cups frozen corn
2 cups frozen diced hash brown potatoes
2 cups chopped green bell peppers
1 teaspoon seafood seasoning
½ teaspoon dried thyme
⅛ teaspoon red pepper flakes (optional)
½ cup milk
2 ounces cream cheese, cut into small pieces
¼ teaspoon salt
Black pepper

1. Bring broth to a boil in large saucepan over high heat. Add corn, hash browns, bell peppers, seafood seasoning, thyme and red pepper flakes, if desired. Return to a boil. Reduce heat; cover. Simmer 15 minutes or until vegetables are tender.

2. Remove from heat. Whisk in milk, cream cheese, salt and black pepper until cream cheese melts. Let stand 5 minutes before serving.

Makes 4 servings

Hash browns are a very versatile and well-loved potato product. They are a staple in diners, usually served with breakfast, alongside a meat entrée, or mixed with leftovers of meat and vegetables for the popular dish known as "hash." They are often formed into cakes, or potato pancakes, and pan-fried or cooked on a griddle.

cream-cheesy garden chowder

potato soup with arugula

2 tablespoons olive oil
2 leeks, white parts only, cleaned and chopped
4 medium potatoes, peeled and diced
3 cups SWANSON® Chicken Broth (Regular, Natural Goodness® or Certified Organic)
1 cup baby arugula
¼ cup heavy cream
2 teaspoons lemon juice

1. Heat the oil in a 4-quart saucepan over medium heat. Add the leeks and cook for 5 minutes. Add the potatoes and cook for 10 minutes or until the potatoes are almost tender.

2. Add the broth. Heat to a boil. Reduce the heat to low. Cover and cook for 20 minutes or until the potatoes are tender. Add the arugula. Cook for 1 minute.

3. Place ½ of the broth mixture into an electric blender or food processor container. Cover and blend until smooth. Pour the mixture into a medium bowl. Repeat the blending process with the remaining broth mixture. Return all of the puréed mixture to the saucepan. Cook over medium heat until the mixture is hot. Season to taste. Stir in the cream and lemon juice. Serve immediately.

Makes 6 servings

Kitchen Tip: This savory soup is also delicious served cold. Refrigerate for at least 3 hours or until well chilled.

Prep Time: 15 minutes
Cook Time: 35 minutes

potato soup with arugula

creamy cauliflower bisque

1 pound cauliflower florets
1 pound russet potatoes, cut into 1-inch pieces
2 cans (about 14 ounces each) reduced-sodium chicken broth
1 cup chopped yellow onion
½ teaspoon dried thyme
¼ teaspoon garlic powder
⅛ teaspoon ground red pepper
1 cup evaporated milk
2 tablespoons butter
½ teaspoon salt
¼ teaspoon black pepper
1 cup (4 ounces) shredded sharp Cheddar cheese
¼ cup finely chopped fresh parsley
¼ cup finely chopped green onions

Slow Cooker Directions

1. Layer cauliflower, potatoes, broth, onion, thyme, garlic powder and red pepper in slow cooker. Cover; cook on LOW 8 hours or on HIGH 4 hours.

2. Working in batches, process soup in blender or food processor until smooth; return to slow cooker. Add evaporated milk, butter, salt and black pepper. Cook, uncovered, on HIGH 30 minutes or until heated through.

3. Top each serving with cheese, parsley and green onions.

Makes 8 servings

potato & spinach soup with gouda

6 cups cubed Yukon Gold potatoes (about 9 medium)
2 cans (about 14 ounces each) chicken broth
½ cup water
1 small red onion, finely chopped
5 ounces baby spinach
½ teaspoon salt
¼ teaspoon ground red pepper
¼ teaspoon black pepper
2½ cups (10 ounces) shredded smoked Gouda cheese, divided
1 can (12 ounces) evaporated milk
1 tablespoon olive oil
4 cloves garlic, cut into thin slices
Chopped fresh parsley

Slow Cooker Directions

1. Combine potatoes, broth, water, onion, spinach, salt, red pepper and black pepper in slow cooker. Cover; cook on LOW 10 hours or on HIGH 4 to 5 hours.

2. *Turn slow cooker to HIGH.* Slightly mash potatoes in slow cooker; add 2 cups cheese and evaporated milk. Cover; cook on HIGH 15 to 20 minutes or until cheese is melted.

3. Heat oil in small skillet over low heat. Add garlic; cook and stir 2 minutes or until golden brown. Sprinkle soup with garlic, remaining ½ cup cheese and parsley.

Makes 8 to 10 servings

chile pepper & corn cream chowder

2 tablespoons butter
1 cup chopped onion
2 Anaheim* or poblano chile peppers, seeded and diced
½ cup thinly sliced celery
1 package (16 ounces) frozen corn
12 ounces unpeeled new red potatoes, diced
4 cups whole milk
6 ounces cream cheese, cubed
2 teaspoons salt
¾ teaspoon black pepper

**Mild, with just the hint of a bite, Anaheim chiles are medium green peppers with a long narrow shape.*

1. Melt butter in large saucepan over medium-high heat. Add onion, Anaheim peppers and celery; cook and stir 5 minutes or until onion is translucent.

2. Add corn, potatoes and milk. Bring to a boil. Reduce heat to medium-low; cover and simmer 10 minutes or until potatoes are tender.

3. Remove from heat; add cream cheese, salt and black pepper. Stir until cream cheese is melted.

Makes 4 to 6 servings

chile pepper & corn cream chowder

blue cheese potato soup with olive tapenade

2 tablespoons olive oil
2 medium onions, chopped (about 1 cup)
5 cloves garlic, minced
6 cups SWANSON® Vegetable Broth (Regular or Certified Organic)
4 pounds red potatoes, peeled and diced
1 tablespoon balsamic vinegar
⅓ cup crumbled blue cheese
½ cup prepared olive tapenade

1. Heat the oil in a 6-quart saucepot over medium heat. Add the onions and garlic and cook until they're tender.

2. Stir the broth and potatoes in the saucepot and heat to a boil. Reduce the heat to low. Cover and cook for 30 minutes or until the potatoes are tender.

3. Pour ⅓ of the broth mixture into a blender or food processor. Cover and blend until smooth. Pour the mixture into a large bowl. Repeat twice more with the remaining broth mixture. Return all of the puréed mixture to the saucepot. Stir in the vinegar and cheese. Increase the heat to medium. Cook for 5 minutes or until the mixture is hot and bubbling. Season as desired.

4. Divide the soup mixture among **12** serving bowls. Top **each** with **2 teaspoons** tapenade.

Makes 12 servings

Kitchen Tip: Serve with a hot crusty French baguette. For dessert serve chocolate mousse pudding.

Prep Time: 20 minutes
Cook Time: 40 minutes

blue cheese potato soup with olive tapenade

two-cheese potato and cauliflower soup

1 tablespoon butter
1 cup chopped onion
2 cloves garlic, minced
5 cups whole milk
1 pound Yukon Gold potatoes, diced
1 pound cauliflower florets
1½ teaspoons salt
⅛ teaspoon ground red pepper
1½ cups (6 ounces) shredded sharp Cheddar cheese
⅓ cup crumbled blue cheese

1. Melt butter in large saucepan over medium-high heat. Add onion; cook and stir 4 minutes or until translucent. Add garlic; cook and stir 15 seconds. Add milk, potatoes, cauliflower, salt and red pepper; bring to a boil. Reduce heat; cover and simmer 15 minutes or until potatoes are tender. Cool slightly.

2. Working in batches, process soup in blender or food processor until smooth. Return to saucepan. Cook and stir over medium heat 2 to 3 minutes or until heated through. Remove from heat; add cheeses. Stir until melted.

Makes 4 to 6 servings

two-cheese potato and cauliflower soup

chile verde chicken stew

⅓ cup all-purpose flour
1½ teaspoons salt, divided
¼ teaspoon black pepper
1½ pounds boneless skinless chicken breasts, cut into 1½-inch pieces
4 tablespoons vegetable oil, divided
1 pound tomatillos (about 9), husked and halved
2 onions, chopped
2 cans (4 ounces each) mild green chiles
1 tablespoon dried oregano
1 tablespoon ground cumin
2 cloves garlic, chopped
1 teaspoon sugar
2 cups reduced-sodium chicken broth
8 ounces Mexican beer
5 red potatoes, diced
Chopped fresh cilantro, sour cream, shredded Monterey Jack cheese, lime wedges, diced avocado and/or hot pepper sauce (optional)

1. Combine flour, 1 teaspoon salt and pepper in large bowl. Add chicken; toss to coat. Heat 2 tablespoons oil in large nonstick skillet over medium heat. Add chicken; cook until lightly browned on all sides, stirring occasionally. Transfer to Dutch oven.

2. Heat remaining 2 tablespoons oil in same skillet. Add tomatillos, onions, chiles, oregano, cumin, garlic, sugar and remaining ½ teaspoon salt. Cook and stir 20 minutes or until vegetables are softened. Stir in broth and beer. Working in batches, process mixture in food processor or blender until almost smooth.

3. Add mixture to Dutch oven; stir in potatoes. Bring to a boil over medium-high heat. Reduce heat to low; simmer, covered, 1 hour or until potatoes are tender, stirring occasionally. Serve with desired toppings.

Makes 6 servings

chile verde chicken stew

peppery potato soup

2 cans (about 14 ounces each) chicken broth
4 small baking potatoes, halved and sliced crosswise
1 large onion, quartered and sliced
1 stalk celery, sliced
½ teaspoon salt
½ teaspoon black pepper, plus additional for serving
1 cup half-and-half
¼ cup all-purpose flour
1 tablespoon butter
Celery leaves and fresh parsley (optional)

Slow Cooker Directions

1. Combine broth, potatoes, onion, celery, salt and ½ teaspoon pepper in slow cooker; mix well. Cover; cook on LOW 6 to 7½ hours.

2. Stir half-and-half into flour in small bowl; stir into slow cooker. Cover; cook 1 hour.

3. Slightly mash potato mixture with potato masher. Cook, uncovered, 30 minutes or until slightly thickened. Just before serving, stir in butter and sprinkle with additional pepper to taste. Garnish with celery leaves and parsley.

Makes 6 servings

Prep Time: 15 minutes
Cook Time: 7½ to 9 hours (LOW)

peppery potato soup

yankee pot roast and vegetables

1 beef chuck pot roast (2½ pounds)
Salt and black pepper
3 unpeeled baking potatoes (about 1 pound), cut into quarters
2 carrots, cut into ¾-inch slices
2 stalks celery, cut into ¾-inch slices
1 onion, sliced
1 parsnip, cut into ¾-inch slices
2 bay leaves
1 teaspoon dried rosemary
½ teaspoon dried thyme
½ cup reduced-sodium beef broth

Slow Cooker Directions

1. Trim and discard excess fat from beef. Cut into ¾-inch pieces; sprinkle with salt and pepper.

2. Combine potatoes, carrots, celery, onion, parsnip, bay leaves, rosemary and thyme in slow cooker. Top with beef. Pour broth over beef. Cover; cook on LOW 8½ to 9 hours or until beef is fork-tender.

3. Transfer beef and vegetables to serving platter. Remove and discard bay leaves.

Makes 10 to 12 servings

Note: To make gravy, ladle the juices into a 2-cup measure; let stand 5 minutes. Skim off fat. Measure remaining juices and heat to a boil in a small saucepan. For each cup of juices, mix 2 tablespoons flour with ¼ cup cold water in a small bowl until smooth; add to boiling juices. Cook and stir constantly 1 minute or until thickened.

Prep Time: 10 minutes
Cook Time: 8½ to 9 hours

meat & potato meals

chili meatloaf and potato bake

1½ pounds ground turkey
¾ cup salsa
1 tablespoon chili powder
1 egg, beaten
1⅓ cups *French's®* French Fried Onions, divided
½ teaspoon salt
¼ teaspoon ground black pepper
2 cups prepared hot mashed potatoes*
2 cups (8 ounces) shredded taco blend cheese, divided

**Prepare instant mashed potatoes for 4 servings.*

1. Preheat oven to 375°F. Combine ground turkey, salsa, chili powder, egg, *⅔ cup* French Fried Onions, salt and pepper until blended. Press turkey mixture into 9-inch square baking dish.

2. Bake 25 minutes or until turkey is cooked through and juices run clear. Drain off fat.

3. Combine potatoes and 1 cup cheese. Spread evenly over meatloaf. Sprinkle with remaining cheese and onions; bake 5 minutes or until cheese is melted and onions are golden. **Makes 6 servings**

Variation: For added Cheddar flavor, substitute ***French's®*** Cheddar French Fried Onions for the original flavor.

Prep Time: 15 minutes
Cook Time: 30 minutes

chili meatloaf and potato bake

ham and sweet potato skillet

2 medium sweet potatoes (about 1¼ pounds)
3 cups water
1 tablespoon salt
1 fully cooked ham steak (about 1 pound)
½ cup brewed coffee
¼ cup pure maple syrup
2 tablespoons butter
½ cup coarsely chopped pecans, toasted*

**To toast pecans, place in a nonstick skillet. Cook and stir over medium-low heat about 5 minutes or until pecans begin to brown. Remove immediately to a plate to cool.*

1. Peel sweet potatoes; cut into ¾-inch pieces. Combine water and salt in large saucepan over medium heat. Add sweet potatoes; simmer 8 to 10 minutes or until almost tender. Drain well.

2. Meanwhile, cut ham into ¾-inch chunks; discard bone and fat.

3. Combine coffee, maple syrup and butter in large skillet. Bring to a boil. Reduce heat; simmer 3 minutes. Add sweet potatoes and ham; simmer, stirring occasionally, until ham is heated through and sauce is bubbly and slightly thickened. Sprinkle with pecans. **Makes 4 servings**

ham and sweet potato skillet

italian-style shepherd's pie

1 pound potatoes, quartered
2 to 3 tablespoons reduced-sodium chicken broth
3 tablespoons grated Parmesan cheese
1 pound ground beef
½ cup chopped onion
2 teaspoons Italian seasoning
¼ teaspoon fennel seeds, crushed (optional)
⅛ teaspoon ground red pepper
2 cups sliced yellow summer squash
1 can (about 14 ounces) chunky pasta-style tomatoes, drained
1 cup corn
⅓ cup tomato paste

1. Preheat oven to 375°F. Combine potatoes and enough water to cover in medium saucepan. Bring to a boil. Boil, uncovered, 20 to 25 minutes or until tender; drain. Mash potatoes, adding enough broth to reach desired consistency. Stir in Parmesan cheese.

2. Brown beef and onion in large skillet over medium-high heat 6 to 8 minutes, stirring to break up meat. Drain fat. Stir in Italian seasoning, fennel seeds, if desired, and red pepper. Add squash, tomatoes, corn and tomato paste; mix well. Spoon mixture into 2-quart casserole. Pipe or spoon potatoes over top.

3. Bake 20 to 25 minutes or until meat mixture is bubbly. Let stand 10 minutes before serving.

Makes 6 servings

italian-style shepherd's pie

bacon onion cornish hens with potatoes

2 *Tyson*® Cornish Game Hen Twin Packs (4 total), thawed
4 strips *Wright*® Brand Bacon, chopped
1 tablespoon cider vinegar
1¾ teaspoons marjoram, divided
1 teaspoon thyme, divided
¾ teaspoon seasoned salt, divided
½ teaspoon dry mustard
4 small potatoes, cut into ¾-inch cubes (about 2½ cups)
1 small onion, cut into wedges
¼ teaspoon garlic-pepper seasoning

1. Set up grill for indirect cooking: For gas grill, preheat all burners on high. Turn one burner off; place food over "off" burner. Reset remaining burner(s) to medium. Close lid. For charcoal grill, arrange hot coals around outer edge of grill. Place disposable pan in open space; place food over open area. Close lid. Heat to medium.

2. Cook bacon in medium skillet over medium-high heat until crisp, stirring frequently. Remove from heat. Transfer bacon and 2 teaspoons drippings to small bowl. Blend vinegar, 1¼ teaspoons marjoram, ¾ teaspoon thyme, ¼ teaspoon seasoned salt and dry mustard into bacon drippings in skillet; cook and stir over medium-low heat until blended.

3. Spray 12×18-inch sheet of heavy-duty aluminum foil lightly with nonstick cooking spray. Toss potatoes, onion, reserved bacon with drippings, remaining ½ teaspoon marjoram, ¼ teaspoon thyme, ½ teaspoon salt and garlic-pepper on foil. Top with 12×18-inch sheet of heavy-duty foil. Fold and crimp edges to seal; allow room for expansion.

4. Wash hands. Rinse hens and pat dry. Secure wings to hens and tie legs together with string, if desired. Rub hens with herb mixture from skillet.

5. Place hens (not touching) over indirect heat on grill. Wash hands. Grill hens, covered, 25 minutes. Place potato packet over hot coals. Grill, covered, 25 to 35 minutes longer, turning potato packet over once, until potatoes are tender and internal juices of chicken run clear. (Or insert instant-read meat thermometer into thickest part of chicken. Temperature should read 180°F.) Refrigerate leftovers immediately.

Makes 4 servings

Prep Time: 35 minutes
Cook Time: 50 minutes
Total Time: 1 hour 25 minutes

bratwurst skillet breakfast

1½ pounds red potatoes
3 bratwurst links (about ¾ pound)
2 tablespoons butter
1½ teaspoons caraway seeds
4 cups shredded red cabbage

1. Cut potatoes into ¼- to ½-inch pieces. Place in microwavable baking dish. Microwave, covered, on HIGH 3 minutes; stir. Microwave 2 minutes more or just until tender.

2. Meanwhile, cut sausage into ¼-inch slices. Cook sausage in large skillet over medium-high heat 8 minutes or until browned and cooked through. Transfer to paper towels; pour off drippings.

3. Melt butter in same skillet. Add potatoes and caraway seeds. Cook, stirring occasionally, 6 to 8 minutes or until potatoes are golden and tender. Return sausage to skillet; stir in cabbage. Cook, covered, 3 minutes or until cabbage is slightly wilted. Uncover; cook and stir 3 to 4 minutes or just until cabbage is tender.

Makes 4 servings

Serving Suggestion: Serve with fresh fruit.

Prep and Cook Time: 30 minutes

chipotle lamb chops with crispy potatoes

4 lamb loin chops
2 teaspoons chipotle chili powder
Salt and black pepper
8 ounces fingerling potatoes
2 tablespoons olive oil
Olive oil cooking spray

1. Rub lamb chops with chili powder. Season with salt and pepper.

2. Cut potatoes into ¼-inch-thick slices. Heat oil in large nonstick skillet over medium heat. Add potatoes, stirring to coat with oil; season with salt and pepper. Cook 15 to 20 minutes or until golden brown and crispy, stirring occasionally.

3. Meanwhile, spray medium nonstick skillet with cooking spray. Add lamb chops. Cook 12 to 15 minutes or until medium rare (145°F), turning once. Serve lamb chops with potatoes. **Makes 2 servings**

tater tip

There is a world of potatoes beyond the basic russet, white and red varieties. Fingerling potatoes, a type of heritage potato that is small and shaped like a finger, are becoming more widely available at large supermarkets and farmers' markets. Search your local market from late summer to early winter for interesting and unusual colors of fingerlings, ranging from buttery yellow to deep fuchsia to vibrant blue and purple.

chipotle lamb chops with crispy potatoes

hearty beef and potato casserole

1 package (about 17 ounces) refrigerated fully cooked beef pot roast in gravy*
3 cups frozen hash brown potatoes
¼ teaspoon salt
¼ teaspoon black pepper
1 can (about 14 ounces) diced tomatoes
½ cup sauce from canned chipotle peppers in adobo sauce
1 cup (4 ounces) shredded sharp Cheddar cheese

**Fully cooked beef pot roast in gravy can be found in the refrigerated prepared meats section of the supermarket.*

1. Preheat oven to 375°F. Lightly coat 11×7-inch glass baking dish with nonstick cooking spray.

2. Drain and discard gravy from pot roast. Cut beef into ¼-inch-thick slices. Place 2 cups potatoes in prepared baking dish. Sprinkle with salt and pepper. Top with beef. Combine tomatoes and adobo sauce in small bowl; spread evenly over beef. Top with remaining 1 cup potatoes. Sprinkle with cheese.

3. Lightly cover dish with foil. Bake 20 minutes. Remove foil; bake 20 minutes or until hot and bubbly. Let stand 5 to 10 minutes before serving.

Makes 6 servings

hearty beef and potato casserole

potato taco lasagna

1 pound lean ground beef
1½ cups chunky salsa
1 package (10 ounces) frozen spinach, thawed, squeezed and drained
¾ cup water
1 package (1.25 ounces) taco seasoning
1 package SIMPLY POTATOES® Homestyle Slices
1½ cups sour cream
3 cups CRYSTAL FARMS® Shredded Cheddar cheese
1 cup corn chips

1. Heat oven to 350°F. In 10-inch skillet, cook ground beef until no longer pink. Drain. Stir in salsa, spinach, water and taco seasoning; set aside.

2. Spray 13×9-inch baking dish with nonstick cooking spray. Place half of the **Simply Potatoes®** on bottom of pan. Top with half of the meat mixture, ¾ cup sour cream and 1½ cups cheese. Repeat layers ending with cheese.

3. Bake, covered, 45 minutes. Uncover; top with corn chips. Continue baking 5 to 10 minutes or until chips are lightly browned. Let stand 10 minutes before cutting. **Makes 12 servings**

Prep Time: 30 minutes
Bake Time: 50 minutes
Standing Time: 10 minutes

potato taco lasagna

rainbow casserole

5 potatoes, cut into thin slices
1 pound ground beef
1 onion, halved and thinly sliced
Salt and black pepper
1 can (about 28 ounces) stewed tomatoes, drained, juice reserved
1 cup frozen peas *or* 1 can (about 6 ounces) peas, drained

1. Preheat oven to 350°F. Lightly coat 3-quart casserole with nonstick cooking spray.

2. Combine potatoes and enough salted water to cover in large saucepan. Bring to a boil. Reduce heat; simmer 15 minutes or until almost tender. Drain.

3. Meanwhile, brown beef in large skillet over medium-high heat 6 to 8 minutes, stirring to break up meat. Drain fat.

4. Layer half of beef, half of potatoes, half of onion, salt, pepper, half of tomatoes and half of peas in prepared casserole. Repeat layers. Add reserved tomato juice.

5. Cover; bake 40 minutes or until most of liquid is absorbed.

Makes 4 to 6 servings

Don't scorn the skin! The skin of potatoes contains a lot of flavor and nutrients, so don't peel potatoes when you don't have to. Even if you plan to peel, cook potatoes with their skins, let them cool slightly and then peel. This will help the potatoes keep some of that good flavor and nutrition. When you know you are going to eat the skin, be sure to scrub them with a vegetable brush to get rid of embedded dirt. In addition to the healthy skin, the flesh of a potato is a good source of fiber, vitamins and minerals, and it is low in calories.

skillet steak & potatoes

2 baking potatoes
1 pound cooked steak or roast beef
2 tablespoons olive oil
1 large onion, chopped
3 cloves garlic, minced
1 teaspoon salt
½ teaspoon black pepper
½ teaspoon paprika
¼ teaspoon red pepper flakes
1 cup corn
1 cup halved grape tomatoes
¼ cup chopped fresh parsley (optional)

1. Poke potatoes with fork. Microwave on HIGH 8 minutes or until they yield to gentle pressure. Cut potatoes and steak into bite-size pieces.

2. Heat oil in large heavy skillet over medium-high heat. Add onion; cook and stir 8 minutes or until beginning to brown. Add garlic; cook and stir 1 minute.

3. Add potatoes; stir to combine. Cook 4 minutes without stirring. Sprinkle with salt, black pepper, paprika and red pepper flakes. Stir, scraping up any browned bits from bottom of skillet. Add corn, tomatoes and steak. Cook and stir until heated through. Garnish with parsley.

Makes 4 servings

skillet steak & potatoes

ham, poblano and potato casserole

¼ cup (½ stick) butter
¼ cup all-purpose flour
1½ cups whole milk
2 pounds baking potatoes, halved and thinly sliced
6 ounces thinly sliced ham, cut into bite-size pieces
1 poblano pepper, cut into thin strips (about 1 cup)
1 cup corn
1 cup chopped red bell pepper
1 cup finely chopped onion
1½ teaspoons salt
¼ teaspoon black pepper
¼ teaspoon ground nutmeg
1½ cups (6 ounces) shredded sharp Cheddar cheese

1. Preheat oven to 350°F. Lightly coat 13×9-inch baking dish with nonstick cooking spray.

2. Melt butter in medium saucepan over medium heat. Add flour; whisk until smooth. Add milk; whisk until smooth. Cook and stir 5 to 7 minutes or until thickened. Remove from heat; set aside.

3. Layer one third of potatoes and half of ham, poblano pepper, corn, bell pepper and onion in prepared baking dish. Sprinkle with half of salt, black pepper and nutmeg. Repeat layers. Top with remaining one third of potatoes. Spoon white sauce evenly over all.

4. Cover with foil; bake 45 minutes. Uncover; bake 30 minutes or until potatoes are tender. Sprinkle with cheese; bake 5 minutes or until cheese is melted. Let stand 15 minutes before serving. **Makes 6 servings**

Note: To make this casserole even easier, use a food processor with the slicing blade attachment to thinly slice potatoes.

ham, poblano and potato casserole

german potato salad with grilled sausage

⅔ cup prepared vinaigrette salad dressing
¼ cup *French's*® Spicy Brown Mustard or *French's*® Honey Dijon Mustard
1 tablespoon sugar
1½ pounds red or other boiling potatoes, cut into ¾-inch cubes
1 teaspoon salt
1 cup chopped green bell pepper
1 cup chopped celery
½ cup chopped onion
½ pound kielbasa or smoked sausage, split lengthwise

1. Combine salad dressing, mustard and sugar in large bowl; set aside.

2. Place potatoes in large saucepan. Add salt and enough water to cover potatoes. Heat to boiling. Cook 10 to 15 minutes until potatoes are tender. Drain and transfer to bowl with dressing. Add bell pepper, celery and onion. Set aside.

3. Grill sausage over medium-high heat until lightly browned and heated through. Cut into small cubes. Add to bowl with potatoes. Toss well to coat evenly. Serve warm.

Makes 6 to 8 servings

Tip: For zesty baked beans, add ½ cup ***French's***® Mustard to 2 (16-ounce) cans pork and beans. Heat and serve.

Prep Time: 15 minutes
Cook Time: 15 minutes

international taters

pasta & potatoes with pesto

3 medium red potatoes, cut into chunks
8 ounces uncooked linguine
¾ cup frozen peas
1 package (about 7 ounces) prepared pesto sauce
¼ cup plus 2 tablespoons grated Parmesan cheese, divided
¼ teaspoon salt
¼ teaspoon black pepper

1. Place potatoes in medium saucepan; cover with water. Bring to a boil over high heat; reduce heat. Cook, uncovered, 10 minutes or until potatoes are tender; drain.

2. Meanwhile, cook linguine according to package directions, adding peas during last 3 minutes of cooking; drain. Return pasta mixture to pan; add potatoes, pesto sauce, ¼ cup cheese, salt and pepper, tossing until blended. Sprinkle with remaining 2 tablespoons cheese.

Makes 6 servings

cabbage colcannon

1 pound new red potatoes, halved
1 tablespoon vegetable oil
1 small onion, thinly sliced
½ small head green cabbage, thinly sliced
Salt and black pepper
3 tablespoons salted butter, divided

1. Place potatoes and enough water to cover in medium saucepan. Bring to a boil. Cook 20 minutes or until tender. Drain well.

2. Heat oil in large nonstick skillet over medium-high heat. Add onion; cook and stir 8 minutes or until onion is lightly browned. Add cabbage; cook and stir 5 minutes or until softened.

3. Add potatoes to skillet; cook until heated through. Slightly mash potatoes. Season to taste with salt and pepper. Place ½ tablespoon slice of butter on each portion just before serving. **Makes 6 servings**

pasta & potatoes with pesto

spanish tapas potatoes (patatas bravas)

2½ pounds small red potatoes, quartered
⅓ cup plus 2 tablespoons olive oil, divided
1 teaspoon coarse or kosher salt
½ teaspoon dried rosemary
1 can (about 14 ounces) diced tomatoes
2 tablespoons red wine vinegar
1 tablespoon minced garlic
1 tablespoon chili powder
1 tablespoon paprika
¼ teaspoon salt
¼ teaspoon chipotle chili powder
⅛ to ¼ teaspoon ground red pepper

1. Preheat oven to 425°F.

2. Combine potatoes, 2 tablespoons oil, coarse salt and rosemary in large bowl; toss to coat. Spread mixture in large shallow baking pan. Roast potatoes 35 to 40 minutes or until crisp and brown, turning every 10 minutes.

3. For sauce, combine tomatoes, remaining ⅓ cup oil, vinegar, garlic, chili powder, paprika, ¼ teaspoon salt, chipotle chili powder and red pepper in blender or food processor. Process just until blended. Transfer to large saucepan. Cover; cook over medium-high heat 5 minutes or until slightly thickened. Cool slightly.

4. To serve, drizzle sauce over potatoes or serve sauce in separate bowl for dipping. **Makes 10 to 12 servings**

Note: Sauce can be made up to 24 hours ahead of time. Cover and refrigerate. Bring to room temperature or reheat before serving.

spanish tapas potatoes (patatas bravas)

fish & chips

¾ cup all-purpose flour
½ cup flat beer or lemon-lime carbonated beverage
Vegetable oil
4 medium russet potatoes, each cut into 8 wedges
Salt
1 egg, separated
1 pound cod fillets (about 6 to 8 small fillets)
Malt vinegar and lemon wedges (optional)

1. Combine flour, beer and 2 teaspoons oil in small bowl. Cover; refrigerate 1 to 2 hours.

2. Pour 2 inches oil into large heavy skillet. Heat over medium heat to 365°F. Add potato wedges in batches. (Do not crowd.) Fry potato wedges 4 to 6 minutes or until browned, turning once. (Allow temperature of oil to return to 365°F between batches.) Drain on paper towels; sprinkle lightly with salt. Reserve oil to fry cod.

3. Stir egg yolk into reserved flour mixture. Beat egg white in medium bowl with electric mixer at medium-high speed until soft peaks form. Fold egg white into flour mixture.

4. Return oil to 365°F. Dip fish pieces into batter in batches; fry 4 to 6 minutes or until batter is crispy and brown and fish begins to flake when tested with fork, turning once. (Allow temperature of oil to return to 365°F between batches.) Drain on paper towels. Serve immediately with potato wedges. Sprinkle with vinegar and serve with lemon wedges, if desired.

Makes 4 servings

fish & chips

potato pierogi

4 medium potatoes (about 1½ pounds), peeled and quartered
⅓ cup milk
2 tablespoons butter
2 tablespoons chopped green onion
1 teaspoon salt, divided
½ teaspoon white pepper, divided
2¾ cups all-purpose flour
1 cup sour cream
1 whole egg
1 egg yolk
1 tablespoon vegetable oil
Melted butter and crumbled cooked bacon
Sour cream (optional)

1. To prepare filling, place potatoes in medium saucepan; cover with water. Bring to a boil. Reduce heat and simmer, uncovered, 20 minutes or until tender; drain.

2. Mash potatoes. Stir in milk, butter, green onion, ½ teaspoon salt and ¼ teaspoon pepper (mixture will be stiff). Cool.

3. To prepare pierogi dough, combine flour, sour cream, whole egg, egg yolk, oil, remaining ½ teaspoon salt and ¼ teaspoon pepper in medium bowl; mix well.

4. Turn out dough onto lightly floured surface. Knead 3 to 5 minutes or until soft and pliable, but not sticky. Let rest, covered, 10 minutes. Divide dough in half. Roll out each half into 13-inch circle on lightly floured surface with lightly floured rolling pin. Cut out circles with 2½-inch round cutter.

5. Place 1 rounded teaspoon potato filling in center of each dough circle. Moisten edges with water. Fold in half; press edges firmly to seal.

6. Bring 4 quarts lightly salted water to a boil in Dutch oven over high heat. Cook pierogi in batches 10 minutes. Remove with slotted spoon to serving dish. Drizzle with butter and top with bacon. Serve with sour cream, if desired.

Makes about 5 dozen pierogi

potato pierogi

swiss onion potatoes rosti

1 tablespoon olive oil
½ cup crumbled cooked bacon
5 cups shredded fresh or frozen potatoes
1⅓ cups *French's*® French Fried Onions
1 cup (4 ounces) shredded Swiss or Cheddar cheese
Applesauce or sour cream (optional)

1. Heat oil in 10-inch nonstick skillet over medium-high heat. Cook bacon 1 minute. Stir in potatoes, French Fried Onions and cheese. Cook 8 minutes or until lightly browned on bottom.

2. Loosen mixture and gently invert onto large serving platter. Return to skillet and cook 6 minutes or until browned.

3. Remove to serving platter. Season to taste with salt and pepper. If desired, serve with dollop of applesauce or sour cream on the side.

Makes 4 to 6 servings

Prep Time: 5 minutes
Cook Time: 15 minutes

tater tip

Rosti is a traditional Swiss dish of shredded potatoes formed into pancakes with a little oil and sautéed until golden. Rosti often has additions such as bacon, onion and cheese. Similar to rosti are latkes, which are traditionally served at Hanukkah and are pancakes of shredded potatoes and eggs. Applesauce and sour cream are typical accompaniments to both.

swiss onion potatoes rosti

spicy african chickpea and sweet potato stew

Spice Paste (recipe follows)
1½ pounds sweet potatoes, peeled and cubed
2 cups vegetable broth or water
1 can (about 15 ounces) chickpeas, rinsed and drained
1 can (about 14 ounces) whole tomatoes, undrained, chopped
1½ cups sliced fresh okra *or* 1 package (10 ounces) frozen cut okra, thawed
Yellow Couscous (page 62)
Hot pepper sauce
Fresh cilantro (optional)

1. Prepare Spice Paste.

2. Combine sweet potatoes, broth, chickpeas, tomatoes with juice, okra and Spice Paste in large saucepan. Bring to a boil over high heat. Reduce heat to low. Cover and simmer 15 minutes. Uncover; simmer 10 minutes or until vegetables are tender.

3. Meanwhile, prepare Yellow Couscous.

4. Serve stew with couscous and hot pepper sauce. Garnish with cilantro.

Makes 4 servings

spice paste

6 cloves garlic
1 teaspoon coarse salt
2 teaspoons paprika
1½ teaspoons whole cumin seeds
1 teaspoon black pepper
½ teaspoon ground ginger
½ teaspoon ground allspice
1 tablespoon olive oil

continued on page 62

spicy african chickpea and sweet potato stew

Process garlic and salt in blender or small food processor until garlic is finely chopped. Add remaining seasonings; process 15 seconds. While blender is running, pour oil through cover opening; process until mixture forms paste.

yellow couscous

1 tablespoon olive oil
5 green onions, sliced
1⅔ cups water
½ teaspoon ground turmeric *or* ⅛ teaspoon saffron threads
¼ teaspoon salt
1 cup uncooked couscous

Heat oil in medium saucepan over medium heat. Add green onions; cook and stir 4 minutes. Add water, turmeric and salt. Bring to a boil; stir in couscous. Remove from heat. Cover; let stand 5 minutes. Fluff with fork.

Makes 3 cups

potato gnocchi with tomato sauce

2 pounds baking potatoes (3 or 4 large)
Tomato Sauce (page 63) or prepared pasta sauce
⅔ to 1 cup all-purpose flour, divided
1 egg yolk
½ teaspoon salt
⅛ teaspoon ground nutmeg (optional)
Grated Parmesan cheese
Slivered fresh basil

1. Preheat oven to 425°F. Pierce potatoes several times with fork. Bake 1 hour or until soft. While potatoes are baking, prepare Tomato Sauce; set aside.

2. Cut potatoes in half lengthwise; cool slightly. Scoop pulp from skins into medium bowl; discard skins. Mash potatoes until smooth. Add ⅓ cup flour, egg yolk, salt and nutmeg, if desired; mix well to form dough.

3. Turn out dough onto well-floured surface. Knead in enough remaining flour to form smooth dough that is not sticky. Divide dough into 4 equal portions. Roll each portion with hands on lightly floured surface into ¾- to 1-inch-wide rope. Cut each rope into 1-inch pieces; gently press thumb into center of each piece to make indentation. Transfer gnocchi to lightly floured kitchen towel in single layer to prevent sticking.

4. Bring 4 quarts salted water to a gentle boil in Dutch oven over high heat. To test gnocchi cooking time, drop several into water; cook 1 minute or until they float to surface. Remove from water with slotted spoon and taste for doneness. (If gnocchi start to dissolve, shorten cooking time by several seconds.) Cook remaining gnocchi in batches, removing with slotted spoon to warm serving dish.

5. Serve gnocchi with Tomato Sauce; sprinkle with cheese and basil.

Makes 4 servings

tomato sauce

2 tablespoons olive oil or butter
1 clove garlic, minced
2 pounds ripe plum tomatoes, peeled, seeded and chopped
1 teaspoon sugar
¼ cup finely chopped prosciutto or cooked ham (optional)
1 tablespoon finely chopped fresh basil
Salt and black pepper

Heat oil in medium saucepan over medium heat. Add garlic; cook 30 seconds or until fragrant. Stir in tomatoes and sugar. Cook 10 minutes or until most of liquid has evaporated. Stir in prosciutto, if desired, and basil. Cook 2 minutes. Season to taste with salt and pepper.

Makes about 2 cups

cauliflower and potato masala

2 tablespoons vegetable oil
1 teaspoon minced garlic
1 teaspoon finely chopped fresh ginger
1 teaspoon salt
1 teaspoon cumin seeds
1 teaspoon ground coriander
1½ cups chopped tomatoes
1 head cauliflower (about 1¼ pounds), broken into florets
8 ounces medium red potatoes, cut into wedges
½ teaspoon garam masala (see Note)
2 tablespoons chopped fresh cilantro

1. Heat oil in large saucepan over medium-high heat. Add garlic, ginger, salt, cumin and coriander; cook and stir about 30 seconds or until fragrant.

2. Add tomatoes; cook and stir 1 minute. Add cauliflower and potatoes; mix well. Reduce heat to low; cover and cook about 30 minutes or until vegetables are tender.

3. Add garam masala; mix well. Sprinkle with cilantro.

Makes 6 servings

Note: Garam masala is an Indian spice mix usually made from coriander, cinnamon, cardamom, black pepper, ginger, nutmeg and other spices. The mix varies according to region and personal preferences. It is available in the spice aisle or at Indian markets.

cauliflower and potato masala

chorizo and papa burritos

14 ounces chorizo sausage
2 small russet potatoes, diced (about 6 ounces)
8 (6-inch) flour tortillas
½ cup (2 ounces) shredded Monterey Jack cheese
¼ cup sour cream

1. Remove chorizo from casing. Crumble chorizo into medium skillet; brown over medium heat 6 to 8 minutes, stirring to separate meat. Add potatoes; cook and stir 12 minutes or until potatoes are tender. Drain fat.

2. Meanwhile, heat tortillas: On gas stove, place tortilla directly onto burner over low flame; turn with tongs when tortilla begins to brown, about 10 seconds. Heat until other side begins to brown. On electric range, preheat burner 2 minutes on medium heat. Place tortilla directly onto burner; turn with tongs when tortilla begins to brown, about 10 seconds. Heat until other side begins to brown.

3. Spoon about ¼ cup chorizo-potato mixture in center of each tortilla. Top with 1 tablespoon cheese and 1½ teaspoons sour cream. Fold bottom of tortillas up over bottom third of filling. Fold in sides of tortillas over filling.

Makes 8 mini burritos

chorizo and papa burritos

portuguese potato & greens soup

2 tablespoons olive oil
1 cup chopped onion
1 cup chopped carrots
2 cloves garlic, minced
1 pound unpeeled new red potatoes, cut into 1-inch pieces
2 cups water
1 can (about 14 ounces) chicken broth
8 ounces chorizo sausage, casing removed
8 ounces kale
Salt and black pepper

1. Heat oil in large saucepan over medium heat. Add onion, carrots and garlic; cook and stir 5 to 6 minutes or until lightly browned. Add potatoes, water and broth. Bring to a boil. Reduce heat to low. Cover; simmer 10 to 15 minutes or until potatoes are tender.

2. Meanwhile, heat large nonstick skillet over medium heat. Crumble chorizo into skillet. Cook and stir 5 to 6 minutes or until cooked through. Drain on paper towels.

3. Wash kale; remove tough stems. Slice into thin shreds.

4. Add chorizo and kale to broth mixture; cook over medium heat 4 to 5 minutes or until heated through. Kale should remain bright green and slightly crunchy. Season with salt and pepper. **Makes 4 servings**

Potatoes and greens are a classic combination wherever potatoes are grown. The English have Bubble and Squeak. The Irish enjoy Colcannon (see page 50 for a recipe). Feel free to choose your own favorite greens for these recipes. Chard, mustard greens, spinach and collards will all work well.

portuguese potato & greens soup

spanish tortilla

1 teaspoon olive oil
1 cup thinly sliced potato
1 small zucchini, thinly sliced
¼ cup chopped onion
1 clove garlic, minced
1 cup shredded cooked chicken
8 eggs
½ teaspoon salt
½ teaspoon black pepper
¼ teaspoon red pepper flakes
Fresh tomato salsa (optional)

1. Heat oil in large nonstick skillet over medium-high heat. Add potato, zucchini, onion and garlic; cook and stir about 5 minutes or until potato is tender. Stir in chicken; cook 1 minute.

2. Meanwhile, whisk eggs, salt, black pepper and red pepper flakes in large bowl. Carefully pour egg mixture into skillet. Reduce heat to low. Cover and cook 12 to 15 minutes or until egg mixture is set in center.

3. Loosen edge of tortilla and slide onto large serving platter. Let stand 5 minutes before cutting into wedges or cubes. Serve warm or at room temperature. Serve with salsa, if desired. **Makes 10 to 12 servings**

tater tip

This tortilla is not your typical tortilla used in Mexican cooking as a wrap for savory fillings. It is a Spanish omelet, or tortilla española, similar to an Italian frittata. It is traditionally made with potatoes, eggs and onions, but you can make any variety of tortilla as you would an omelet. It is excellent for all meals of the day or as a tapa, and it can be served warm, cool or at room temperature. Use a low-starch potato for this recipe, such as a red potato or Yukon Gold.

spanish tortilla

spicy steak fries

2 large potatoes
2 tablespoons MRS. DASH® Extra Spicy Seasoning Blend
2 tablespoons olive oil
1 clove garlic, minced

1. Preheat oven to 425°F. Wash and cut potatoes into wedges; do not peel. Dry potato slices on paper towels.

2. In a large bowl, toss potatoes with MRS. DASH® Extra Spicy Seasoning Blend, olive oil and garlic.

3. Spray baking sheet with nonstick cooking spray and lay wedges on baking sheet. Bake potatoes for 20 minutes. Turn the potatoes and bake another 15 minutes or until potatoes are browned and tender.

Makes 4 servings

Prep Time: 10 minutes
Cook Time: 35 to 40 minutes

mashed, fried & on the side

creamy golden mushroom mashed potatoes

6 medium baking potatoes, cut into 1-inch pieces (about 6 cups)
1 small onion, cut into wedges
Water
1 can (10¾ ounces) CAMPBELL'S® Condensed Golden Mushroom Soup
¾ cup milk
¼ cup heavy cream
4 tablespoons butter

1. Put the potatoes and onion in a 4-quart saucepot with enough water to cover them. Heat the potatoes over medium-high heat to a boil. Reduce the heat to low. Cover and cook the potatoes for 20 minutes or until they're fork-tender. Drain the potatoes and onion well in a colander.

2. Put the potatoes and onion in a 3-quart bowl and beat with an electric mixer at medium speed until almost smooth.

3. Put the soup, milk, cream and butter in a 4-cup microwavable measuring cup. Microwave on HIGH for 2½ minutes or until hot. Slowly pour the hot soup mixture into the potatoes, beating with an electric mixer at medium speed until the potatoes are smooth. Season to taste.

Makes 6 servings

Prep Time: 20 minutes
Cook Time: 30 minutes

creamy golden mushroom mashed potatoes

NATIONAL
MUSEUM
OF THE
AMERICAN
INDIAN

baked sweet potato fries with spicy apricot dipping sauce

3 sweet potatoes (12 to 14 ounces each), peeled and cut into narrow wedges
2 tablespoons vegetable oil
1½ teaspoons coarse or kosher salt
¼ teaspoon black pepper
Spicy Apricot Dipping Sauce (recipe follows)

1. Preheat oven to 450°F. Gently toss potatoes, oil, salt and pepper in large bowl until potatoes are evenly coated. Divide potatoes between 2 large baking sheets or jelly-roll pans. Bake 30 minutes or until tender and lightly browned.

2. Meanwhile, prepare Spicy Apricot Dipping Sauce. Serve with hot potatoes.

Makes 6 servings

spicy apricot dipping sauce

1 cup apricot jam
¼ cup orange juice
1 tablespoon prepared mustard
¼ teaspoon ground red pepper

Melt jam in small saucepan over medium-high heat. Whisk in orange juice, mustard and red pepper. Purée sauce in food processor or with immersion blender, if desired.

Makes 6 servings

Tip: Sauce can also be served with chicken, either as a dipping sauce, or brushed over cooked chicken and browned briefly under the broiler for a tasty glaze.

baked sweet potato fries with spicy apricot dipping sauce

parmesan potato wedges

2 pounds red potatoes, cut into ½-inch wedges
¼ cup finely chopped yellow onion
1½ teaspoons dried oregano
½ teaspoon salt
Black pepper
2 tablespoons butter, cut into small pieces
¼ cup grated Parmesan cheese

Slow Cooker Directions

Layer potatoes, onion, oregano, salt, pepper and butter in slow cooker. Cover; cook on HIGH 4 hours. Transfer potatoes to serving platter and sprinkle with cheese. **Makes 6 servings**

Prep Time: 10 minutes
Cook Time: 4 hours (HIGH)

creamy smashed red potatoes with cheese

3 pounds new red potatoes, unpeeled, cut into quarters
1 cup or more NESTLÉ® CARNATION® Evaporated Lowfat 2% Milk
2 tablespoons butter, cut into pieces
¾ cup grated Parmesan cheese blend
Salt and ground black pepper to taste

PLACE potatoes in large saucepan. Cover with water; bring to a boil. Cook over medium-high heat for 15 to 20 minutes or until potatoes are tender; drain.

RETURN potatoes to saucepan. Beat with hand-held mixer for a few seconds to break up. Add evaporated milk and butter; beat until milk and butter are mixed in (some lumps will still be present). Add additional evaporated milk if a smoother consistency is desired. Stir in cheese. Season with salt and pepper to taste. **Makes 15 (½-cup) servings**

parmesan potato wedges

lemon-mint red potatoes

2 pounds new red potatoes
3 tablespoons olive oil
1 teaspoon salt
¾ teaspoon Greek seasoning or dried oregano
¼ teaspoon garlic powder
¼ teaspoon black pepper
1 teaspoon grated lemon peel
2 tablespoons lemon juice
2 tablespoons butter
4 tablespoons chopped fresh mint, divided

Slow Cooker Directions

1. Coat inside of 6-quart slow cooker with nonstick cooking spray. Add potatoes and oil, stirring gently to coat. Sprinkle with salt, Greek seasoning, garlic powder and pepper. Cover; cook on LOW 7 hours or on HIGH 4 hours.

2. Stir in lemon peel, lemon juice, butter and 2 tablespoons mint until butter is completely melted. Cover; cook 15 minutes to allow flavors to blend. Sprinkle with remaining 2 tablespoons mint just before serving.

Makes 4 servings

Tip: Potatoes can stand, covered, at room temperature for up to 2 hours.

Prep Time: 25 minutes
Cook Time: 7¼ hours (LOW) or 4¼ hours (HIGH)

lemon-mint red potatoes

chive & onion mashed potatoes

2 pounds potatoes, peeled, quartered (about 6 cups)
½ cup milk
1 tub (8 ounces) PHILADELPHIA® Chive & Onion Cream Cheese Spread
¼ cup KRAFT® Ranch Dressing

PLACE potatoes and enough water to cover in 3-quart saucepan. Bring to a boil.

REDUCE heat to medium; cook 20 to 25 minutes or until tender. Drain.

MASH potatoes, gradually stirring in milk, cream cheese spread and dressing until light and fluffy. Serve immediately.

Makes 10 servings, ½ cup each

Make Ahead: Mix ingredients as directed; spoon into 1½-quart casserole dish. Cover. Refrigerate several hours or overnight. When ready to serve, bake, uncovered, at 350°F 1 hour or until heated through.

Substitute: Substitute KRAFT® Three Cheese Ranch Dressing for Ranch Dressing.

Prep Time: 10 minutes
Cook Time: 25 minutes

peasant potatoes

¼ cup (½ stick) butter
1 large onion, chopped
2 cloves garlic, chopped
8 ounces smoked beef sausage, cut into ¾-inch slices
1 teaspoon dried oregano
6 medium Yukon Gold potatoes, cut into 2-inch pieces
Salt and black pepper
2 cups sliced savoy or other cabbage
1 cup diced roasted red bell peppers
½ cup grated Parmesan cheese

Slow Cooker Directions

1. Melt butter in large skillet over medium heat. Add onion and garlic; cook and stir 5 minutes or until onion is translucent. Add sausage and oregano; cook and stir 5 minutes. Stir in potatoes, salt and black pepper. Transfer mixture to slow cooker.

2. Cover; cook on LOW 6 to 8 hours or on HIGH 3 to 4 hours, stirring every hour. Add cabbage and bell peppers during last 30 minutes of cooking.

3. Top with Parmesan cheese before serving. **Makes 6 servings**

roasted peppers and potatoes

2 pounds small red potatoes, quartered
1 large red bell pepper, cut into 1½-inch chunks
1 large yellow or orange bell pepper, cut into 1½-inch chunks
1 large red onion, cut into 1-inch pieces
¼ cup olive oil
3 cloves garlic, minced
¾ teaspoon salt
¼ teaspoon black pepper
¼ teaspoon dried basil
¼ teaspoon dried oregano

1. Preheat oven to 375°F.

2. Place potatoes, bell peppers and onion in large resealable food storage bag. Combine oil, garlic, salt, black pepper, basil and oregano in small bowl; pour over vegetables in bag. Seal; shake until vegetables are evenly coated. Spread on large baking sheet.

3. Bake 50 minutes or until potatoes are tender and beginning to brown, stirring every 15 minutes. **Makes 4 to 6 servings**

Store potatoes in a cool, dark, well-ventilated place (light and warmth encourage sprouting) for up to two weeks. Check them occasionally and remove any that have sprouted or begun to shrivel. One rotten potato can spoil the whole lot. Avoid storing potatoes and onions together as the gases given off by the onions can cause the potatoes to spoil more quickly. Avoid storing potatoes in the refrigerator as the starch turns to sugar, making them overly sweet.

roasted peppers and potatoes

new potatoes and peas

9 small new potatoes, cut into quarters (about 1½ pounds)
1 can (10¾ ounces) CAMPBELL'S® Condensed Cream of Mushroom Soup (Regular or 98% Fat Free)
⅓ cup milk
½ teaspoon dried thyme leaves or dill weed, crushed
⅛ teaspoon ground black pepper
1 package (10 ounces) frozen peas or peas with pearl onions, thawed and drained

1. Place the potatoes in a 4-quart saucepan. Cover the potatoes with water. Heat over high heat to a boil. Reduce the heat to medium. Cook for 8 minutes or until the potatoes are fork-tender. Drain the potatoes in a colander.

2. In the same saucepan, stir the soup, milk, thyme and black pepper. Stir in the potatoes and peas. Heat over low heat, stirring occasionally until heated through.

Makes 7 servings

Prep Time: 10 minutes
Cook Time: 20 minutes

potato-cauliflower mash

3 cups water
2 cups cubed Yukon Gold potatoes (about 12 ounces)
10 ounces frozen cauliflower florets
¼ cup evaporated milk
2 tablespoons butter
¾ teaspoon salt
¼ teaspoon black pepper

1. Bring water to a boil in large saucepan. Add potatoes and cauliflower; return to a boil. Reduce heat; cover and simmer 10 minutes or until potatoes are tender.

2. Drain vegetables; add evaporated milk, butter, salt and pepper. Mash until smooth.

Makes 4 servings

new potatoes and peas

vegetable casserole

2 packages (10 ounces each) frozen spinach
¾ cup (1½ sticks) butter, divided
Salt and black pepper
8 potatoes, cooked until tender
1 cup milk
1 pound carrots, sliced and cooked until tender
1 pound green beans, cut into 1-inch pieces and cooked until tender
½ teaspoon paprika

1. Preheat oven to 375°F. Lightly grease 4-quart casserole or roasting pan.

2. Cook spinach according to package directions; drain and squeeze dry. Spread spinach in prepared casserole; dot with 1 tablespoon butter and season with salt and pepper.

3. Mash potatoes with milk and ½ cup butter in large bowl until creamy.

4. Layer half of potatoes, carrots and green beans over spinach. Dot with another 1 tablespoon butter; season with salt and pepper. Top with remaining potatoes. Dot with remaining 2 tablespoons butter and sprinkle with paprika.

5. Bake 1 hour or until heated through and lightly browned.

Makes 10 to 12 servings

vegetable casserole

zippy oven fries

1 pound russet potatoes, sliced into ¼-inch wedges
3 tablespoons melted butter or vegetable oil
2 tablespoons *Frank's® RedHot®* Original Cayenne Pepper Sauce, at room temperature
2 cups *French's®* French Fried Onions, finely crushed
½ cup grated Parmesan cheese
Zestup Ketchup (recipe follows)

1. Preheat oven to 400°F. Place potatoes, butter and ***Frank's RedHot*** Sauce in large resealable plastic bag. Seal bag and toss potatoes to coat.

2. Combine French Fried Onions and cheese on sheet of waxed paper. Coat potatoes in crumb mixture, pressing firmly.

3. Arrange potatoes in single layer in shallow baking pan coated with nonstick cooking spray. Bake, uncovered, 25 minutes or until potatoes are tender and golden brown. Splash on more ***Frank's RedHot*** Sauce or serve with Zestup Ketchup.

Makes 4 servings

Zestup Ketchup: Combine 1 cup ketchup with 1 to 2 tablespoons ***Frank's RedHot*** Sauce.

Prep Time: 10 minutes
Cook Time: 25 minutes

zippy oven fries

chunky ranch potatoes

3 pounds medium red potatoes, quartered
1 cup water
½ cup prepared ranch dressing
½ cup grated Parmesan or Cheddar cheese (optional)
¼ cup minced chives

Slow Cooker Directions

1. Place potatoes in slow cooker; add water. Cover; cook on LOW 7 to 9 hours or on HIGH 4 to 6 hours or until potatoes are tender.

2. Stir in ranch dressing, cheese, if desired, and chives. Break up potatoes into chunks.

Makes 8 servings

Prep Time: 10 minutes
Cook Time: 7 to 9 hours (LOW) or 4 to 6 hours (HIGH)

garlic fries

1 envelope LIPTON® RECIPE SECRETS® Savory Herb with Garlic Soup Mix*
1 cup plain dry bread crumbs
2 pounds large red or all-purpose potatoes, cut lengthwise into wedges
⅓ cup I CAN'T BELIEVE IT'S NOT BUTTER!® Spread, melted

**Also terrific with LIPTON® RECIPE SECRETS® Onion Soup Mix.*

1. Preheat oven to 400°F. In large bowl, blend soup mix with bread crumbs. Dip potatoes in I Can't Believe It's Not Butter!® Spread, then soup mixture, until evenly coated.

2. In 15½×10½×1-inch jelly-roll pan sprayed with nonstick cooking spray, arrange potatoes in single layer.

3. Bake uncovered 40 minutes or until potatoes are tender and golden brown.

Makes 4 servings

chunky ranch potatoes

bacon and cheese brunch potatoes

3 medium russet potatoes (about 2 pounds), cut into 1-inch pieces
1 cup chopped onion
½ teaspoon seasoned salt
4 slices bacon, crisp-cooked and crumbled
1 cup (4 ounces) shredded sharp Cheddar cheese
1 tablespoon water or chicken broth

Slow Cooker Directions

1. Coat slow cooker with nonstick cooking spray. Layer half of potatoes, onion, seasoned salt, bacon and cheese in slow cooker. Repeat layers, ending with cheese. Sprinkle water over top.

2. Cover; cook on LOW 6 hours or on HIGH 3½ hours or until potatoes and onion are tender. Stir gently to mix and serve hot.

Makes 6 servings

Prep Time: 10 minutes
Cook Time: 6 hours (LOW) or 3½ hours (HIGH)

stuffed, baked & roasted

swiss-style twice baked potatoes

4 large evenly shaped baking potatoes (about 2½ pounds)
4 teaspoons butter, softened
⅔ cup grated Emmentaler cheese*
⅔ cup grated Gruyère cheese*
½ teaspoon caraway seeds (optional)
4 teaspoons dry white wine
2 teaspoons kirsch (cherry brandy, optional)
½ teaspoon minced garlic
½ teaspoon salt

**Emmentaler and Gruyère are imported Swiss cheeses that are aged longer than domestic Swiss. Any Swiss cheese can be used.*

1. Preheat oven to 425°F. Scrub potatoes; dry well. Rub each potato with 1 teaspoon butter. Pierce potatoes several times with fork. Place in shallow baking dish at least 1 inch apart. Bake 50 to 60 minutes or until tender. Cool for several minutes.

2. Meanwhile, combine cheeses and caraway seeds, if desired, in small bowl. Set aside.

3. Cut off top third of potatoes. Scoop out potato pulp from bottom sections leaving ¼-inch shell. Place pulp in large bowl, reserving shells. Add pulp from potato tops to bowl; discard top skins.

4. Mash pulp until smooth. Add wine, kirsch, if desired, garlic and salt; mash to blend. Stir in cheese mixture; mash lightly until well blended. Spoon mixture into potato shells, mounding evenly.

5. Place potatoes in baking dish. Bake 20 to 25 minutes or until tops are lightly browned and potatoes are heated through. **Makes 4 servings**

swiss-style twice baked potatoes

taco-topped potatoes

4 baking potatoes (about 6 ounces each), scrubbed and pierced with fork
8 ounces ground beef
½ package (1¼ ounces) taco seasoning mix
½ cup water
1 cup diced tomatoes
¼ teaspoon salt
2 cups shredded lettuce
½ cup (2 ounces) shredded sharp Cheddar cheese
Chopped green onions
Sour cream

1. Microwave potatoes on HIGH 6 to 7 minutes or until fork-tender.

2. Brown beef in large nonstick skillet over medium-high heat 6 to 8 minutes, stirring to break up meat. Drain fat. Add seasoning mix and water; stir to blend. Cook 1 minute. Remove from heat.

3. Toss tomatoes with salt in medium bowl.

4. Split potatoes almost in half and fluff with fork. Fill with equal amounts of beef mixture. Top with tomatoes, lettuce, cheese and green onions. Serve with sour cream.

Makes 4 servings

taco-topped potato

thyme-scented roasted sweet potatoes and onions

2 unpeeled large sweet potatoes (about 1¼ pounds), scrubbed
1 medium sweet or yellow onion, cut into chunks
2 tablespoons canola oil
1 teaspoon dried thyme
½ teaspoon salt
½ teaspoon smoked paprika
⅛ teaspoon ground red pepper (optional)

1. Preheat oven to 425°F. Spray 15×10-inch jelly-roll pan with nonstick cooking spray.

2. Cut sweet potatoes into 1-inch chunks; place in large bowl. Add onion, oil, thyme, salt, paprika and red pepper, if desired; toss to coat. Spread vegetables in single layer on prepared pan.

3. Bake 20 to 25 minutes or until very tender, stirring after 10 minutes. Let stand 5 minutes before serving. **Makes 6 to 8 servings**

Sweet potatoes come in many varieties, but despite their resemblance to yams, the two are unrelated. Rich in vitamin A, vitamin C and minerals, they pack more nutrition than white potatoes. Their sweetness is due to a remarkably high sugar content that is increased even further during cooking. Extremely versatile, sweet potatoes can be roasted, boiled, baked, stuffed, mashed, candied and made into puddings, casseroles and pies.

thyme-scented roasted sweet potatoes and onions

mexican hash brown bake

Nonstick cooking spray
1 container (13 ounces) ORTEGA® Salsa & Cheese Bowl
1½ cups sour cream
1 can (4 ounces) ORTEGA® Fire-Roasted Diced Green Chiles or Diced Jalapeños
1 package (30 ounces) frozen shredded hash brown potatoes
2 ORTEGA® Taco Shells, coarsely crushed

PREHEAT oven to 350°F. Spray 13×9-inch baking dish with cooking spray.

COMBINE Salsa & Cheese, sour cream and chiles in large bowl; stir until blended. Gently stir in hash browns. Spoon mixture into baking dish.

SPRINKLE with crushed taco shells.

BAKE for 45 to 50 minutes or until bubbly around edges. Let stand for 5 minutes before serving. **Makes 12 servings (1 cup each)**

Tip: Make this dish extra special by adding two sliced green onions or two slices crisp, crumbled bacon.

oven-roasted root vegetables

Vegetable cooking spray
3 medium red potatoes, cut into 1-inch pieces
2 cups fresh or frozen whole baby carrots
1 pound celery root (celeriac), peeled and cut into 1-inch pieces
1 rutabaga, peeled and cut into 1-inch pieces
2 medium red onions, cut into 8 wedges each
2 medium parsnips, peeled and cut into 1-inch pieces
5 cloves garlic, cut into thin slices
1 tablespoon chopped fresh rosemary leaves or chopped fresh thyme leaves
1 tablespoon olive oil
1 cup SWANSON® Chicken Broth

1. Heat the oven to 425°F. Spray a 17×11-inch roasting pan or shallow baking sheet with the cooking spray.

2. Stir the potatoes, carrots, celery root, rutabaga, onions, parsnips, garlic, rosemary and oil in the prepared pan. Roast the vegetables for 30 minutes. Pour the broth over the vegetables and stir.

3. Roast for 20 minutes more or until the vegetables are fork-tender.

Makes 8 servings

Prep Time: 30 minutes
Cook Time: 50 minutes

savory herb roasted potatoes

2 pounds red potatoes, cut into wedges (about 6 medium)
1⅓ cups *French's*® Cheddar French Fried Onions or *French's*® French Fried Onions
¼ cup parsley, minced
6 cloves garlic, halved
6 sprigs thyme or rosemary
2 tablespoons olive oil
1 teaspoon salt
¼ teaspoon ground black pepper
2 ice cubes
1 large foil oven roasting bag

1. Toss all ingredients in large bowl. Open foil bag; spoon potatoes into bag in an even layer. Seal bag with tight double folds. Place bag on baking sheet.

2. Place bag on grill over medium-high heat. Cover grill and cook 25 minutes until potatoes are tender, turning bag over once.

3. Return bag to baking sheet and carefully cut top of bag open. Sprinkle with additional French Fried Onions, if desired. **Makes 4 to 6 servings**

Note: Too cold for outdoor grilling? Bake these potatoes in a 450°F oven for 25 to 30 minutes.

Prep Time: 10 minutes
Cook Time: 25 minutes

gratin of two potatoes

2 large baking potatoes (about 1¼ pounds)
2 large sweet potatoes (about 1¼ pounds)
1 tablespoon butter
1 large onion, thinly sliced and separated into rings
2 teaspoons all-purpose flour
1 cup reduced-sodium chicken broth
½ teaspoon salt
¼ teaspoon white pepper *or* ⅛ teaspoon ground red pepper
¾ cup grated Parmesan cheese

1. Cook baking potatoes in large pot of boiling water 10 minutes. Add sweet potatoes; return to a boil. Simmer potatoes, uncovered, 25 minutes or until tender. Drain; cool under cold running water.

2. Meanwhile, melt butter in large nonstick skillet over medium heat. Add onion; cook and stir 10 to 12 minutes or until tender. Sprinkle with flour; cook and stir 1 minute. Add broth, salt and pepper; bring to a boil. Reduce heat; simmer, uncovered, 2 minutes or until sauce thickens, stirring occasionally.

3. Preheat oven to 375°F. Spray 13×9-inch baking dish with nonstick cooking spray. Peel potatoes; cut crosswise into ¼-inch slices. Layer half of baking and sweet potato slices in prepared dish. Spoon half of onion mixture evenly over potatoes. Repeat layers.

4. Cover with foil; bake 25 minutes or until heated through. Preheat broiler. Uncover potatoes; sprinkle evenly with cheese. Broil, 5 inches from heat, 3 to 4 minutes or until cheese is bubbly and light golden brown.

Makes 6 servings

gratin of two potatoes

mediterranean-style roasted vegetables

1½ pounds red potatoes
1 tablespoon plus 1½ teaspoons olive oil, divided
1 red bell pepper
1 yellow or orange bell pepper
1 small red onion
2 cloves garlic, minced
½ teaspoon salt
¼ teaspoon black pepper
1 tablespoon balsamic vinegar
¼ cup chopped fresh basil leaves

1. Preheat oven to 425°F. Spray large shallow roasting pan with nonstick cooking spray. Cut potatoes into 1½-inch chunks; place in prepared pan. Drizzle 1 tablespoon oil over potatoes; toss to coat. Bake 10 minutes.

2. Cut bell peppers into 1½-inch pieces. Cut onion into ½-inch wedges. Add bell peppers and onion to pan. Drizzle remaining 1½ teaspoons oil over vegetables; sprinkle with garlic, salt and black pepper. Toss well to coat. Bake 18 to 20 minutes or until vegetables are browned and tender, stirring once.

3. Transfer to large serving bowl. Drizzle vinegar over vegetables; toss to coat. Add basil; toss again. Serve warm or at room temperature.

Makes 6 servings

mediterranean-style roasted vegetables

easy cheesy potatoes

WHAT YOU NEED

1 pound russet potatoes (about 4 medium), cut into ½-inch chunks

½ pound (8 ounces) VELVEETA® Pasteurized Prepared Cheese Product, cut up

½ cup chopped onions

¼ cup KRAFT® Real Mayo Mayonnaise

4 slices OSCAR MAYER® Bacon, cooked, drained and crumbled (about ¼ cup)

MAKE IT

HEAT oven to 375°F. Combine all ingredients except bacon in 8-inch square baking dish sprayed with cooking spray; cover with foil.

BAKE 45 minutes.

TOP with bacon; bake, uncovered, 5 to 10 minutes or until potatoes are tender.

Makes 10 servings, ½ cup each

Special Extra: Sprinkle with 1 tablespoon chopped fresh parsley just before serving.

Prep Time: 15 minutes
Total Time: 1 hour 10 minutes

two-toned stuffed potatoes

3 large baking potatoes (12 ounces each)
2 large sweet potatoes (12 ounces each), dark flesh preferred
3 slices thick-cut bacon, cut in half
2 cups chopped onions
⅔ cup buttermilk
¼ cup (½ stick) butter, cut into small pieces
¾ teaspoon salt, divided

1. Preheat oven to 450°F. Pierce potatoes with fork in several places. Bake directly on rack 45 minutes or until fork-tender. Let potatoes stand until cool enough to handle. *Reduce oven temperature to 350°F.*

2. Meanwhile, cook bacon in medium skillet over medium-high heat 6 to 8 minutes or until crisp. Remove from heat; transfer bacon to paper towels.

3. Add onions to drippings in skillet; cook and stir about 12 minutes over medium-high heat or until golden brown. Remove onions to small bowl. Stir buttermilk into skillet, scraping up browned bits from bottom of pan. Add butter; stir until melted.

4. Cut baking potatoes in half lengthwise. Scoop out flesh into large bowl, reserving ¼-inch-thick shells. Add three fourths of buttermilk mixture, three fourths of onions and ½ teaspoon salt. Mash with potato masher until smooth.

5. Cut sweet potatoes in half lengthwise. Scoop out flesh into medium bowl. Discard skins. Add remaining buttermilk mixture, onions and ¼ teaspoon salt to sweet potatoes. Mash with potato masher until smooth.

6. Fill half of each potato skin with baked potato mixture; fill other half with sweet potato mixture. Top each with bacon slice. Transfer stuffed potatoes to baking sheet; bake 15 minutes or until heated through.

Makes 6 servings

Tip: These stuffed potatoes can be made and frozen weeks in advance. Reheat the frozen potatoes in a preheated 350°F oven 75 to 90 minutes. If the potatoes are made ahead and refrigerated for a few days, reheat them in a preheated 350°F oven about 25 minutes.

two-toned stuffed potatoes

scalloped potato-onion bake

1 can (10¾ ounces) CAMPBELL'S® Condensed Cream of Celery Soup (Regular or 98% Fat Free)
½ cup milk
Dash ground black pepper
4 medium potatoes (about 1¼ pounds), thinly sliced
1 small onion, thinly sliced (about ¼ cup)
1 tablespoon butter, cut into pieces
Paprika

1. Stir the soup, milk and black pepper with a whisk or fork in a small bowl. Layer half of the potatoes, half of the onion and half of the soup mixture in a 1½-quart casserole. Repeat the layers. Place the butter over the soup mixture. Sprinkle with the paprika. Cover the dish with foil.

2. Bake at 400°F. for 1 hour. Uncover and bake for 15 minutes more or until the potatoes are fork-tender. **Makes 6 servings**

Prep Time: 10 minutes
Bake Time: 1 hour 15 minutes

Scallop refers to the technique of preparing a food, most often potatoes, by slicing it into thin pieces, layering it in a casserole with a creamy sauce and baking until hot and bubbly. The dish may be topped with cracker or bread crumbs before baking for a crunchy twist.

scalloped potato-onion bake

NATIONAL
MUSEUM
OF THE
AMERICAN
INDIAN

potato, beer and cheese gratin

1 bottle (12 ounces) light-colored beer
2 sprigs fresh thyme
1 bay leaf
½ cup whipping cream
1 tablespoon all-purpose flour
2 cloves garlic, minced
2 pounds potatoes (about 3 large), scrubbed and sliced
1 teaspoon salt
1 teaspoon black pepper
2 cups (8 ounces) shredded Gruyère or Emmentaler cheese
2 tablespoons chopped chives (optional)

1. Bring beer, thyme and bay leaf to a boil in medium saucepan. Reduce heat. Cook, stirring frequently, 5 minutes or until liquid reduces to ¾ cup. Remove thyme and bay leaf. Let cool.

2. Combine cream, flour and garlic in small bowl; mix well. Stir into cooled beer mixture.

3. Preheat oven to 375°F. Butter 13×9-inch baking dish. Arrange half of potato slices in bottom of prepared dish, overlapping slightly. Sprinkle with salt and pepper. Pour half of cream-beer mixture over potatoes; sprinkle with half of cheese. Repeat layers.

4. Cover; bake 30 minutes. *Reduce oven temperature to 350°F.* Uncover; bake about 30 minutes or until potatoes are tender when poked with knife and top is golden brown. Let stand 10 minutes before serving. Garnish with chives.

Makes 8 servings

Variation: Add 1 teaspoon of minced jalapeño pepper to the gratin to add extra spice and balance the taste of the beer. Add the jalapeño with the cheese while building the gratin layers in step 3.

potato, beer and cheese gratin

roasted red potato bites

1½ pounds red potatoes (about 15 small)
1 cup shredded Cheddar cheese (about 4 ounces)
½ cup HELLMANN'S® or BEST FOODS® Real Mayonnaise
½ cup sliced green onions
10 slices bacon, crisp-cooked and crumbled
2 tablespoons chopped fresh basil leaves (optional)

1. Preheat oven to 400°F. On large baking sheet, arrange potatoes and bake 35 minutes or until tender. Let stand until cool enough to handle.

2. Cut each potato in half, then cut thin slice from bottom of each potato half. With small melon baller or spoon, scoop pulp from potatoes leaving ¼-inch shell. Place pulp in medium bowl; set shells aside.

3. Lightly mash pulp. Stir in remaining ingredients. Spoon or pipe potato filling into potato shells.

4. Arrange filled shells on baking sheet and broil 3 minutes or until golden and heated through.

Makes 30 bites

Prep Time: 10 minutes
Cook Time: 40 minutes

salads, snacks & more

picnic potato salad

2 pounds red potatoes
⅓ to ½ cup mayonnaise
⅓ cup sour cream
2 to 3 tablespoons spicy brown or coarse grain mustard
¾ teaspoon salt
¼ teaspoon black pepper
2 hard-cooked eggs, chopped
½ cup crisp-cooked and crumbled bacon
¼ cup chopped fresh chives
Additional crisp-cooked and crumbled bacon and chives (optional)

1. Place potatoes in large saucepan; cover with water. Bring to a boil over high heat. Reduce heat to low; simmer, covered, 20 to 25 minutes or until tender. Drain; cool under cold running water.

2. Meanwhile, combine mayonnaise, sour cream, mustard, salt and pepper in large bowl; mix well.

3. Cut potatoes into chunks; add to mayonnaise mixture. Add eggs, bacon and chives; toss gently. Cover; refrigerate at least 2 hours or up to 24 hours. Just before serving, garnish with additional bacon and chives.

Makes 8 to 10 servings

picnic potato salad

tex-mex potato skins

3 hot baked potatoes, split lengthwise
¾ cup (3 ounces) shredded Cheddar or pepper Jack cheese
1⅓ cups *French's*® French Fried Onions, divided
¼ cup chopped green chilies
¼ cup crumbled cooked bacon
Salsa and sour cream

1. Preheat oven to 350°F. Scoop out inside of potatoes, leaving ¼-inch shells. Reserve inside of potatoes for another use.

2. Arrange potato halves on baking sheet. Top with cheese, *⅔ cup* French Fried Onions, chilies and bacon.

3. Bake 15 minutes or until heated through and cheese is melted. Cut each potato half crosswise into thirds. Serve topped with salsa, sour cream and remaining onions. **Makes 18 appetizer servings**

Tip: To bake potatoes quickly, microwave at HIGH 10 to 12 minutes or until tender.

Variation: For added Cheddar flavor, substitute ***French's***® Cheddar French Fried Onions for the original flavor.

Prep Time: 15 minutes
Cook Time: 15 minutes

tex-mex potato skins

traditional german potato salad

2½ pounds red potatoes
¼ pound bacon, cut into small pieces
½ medium onion, finely chopped
½ cup cider vinegar
¼ cup water
1 tablespoon plus 1 teaspoon sugar
1 teaspoon salt
1 teaspoon brown mustard seeds
1 teaspoon prepared mustard
2 tablespoons finely chopped fresh parsley
1 teaspoon paprika

1. Place potatoes in large saucepan. Add enough water to cover. Bring to a boil over high heat. Reduce heat and simmer, uncovered, 20 to 30 minutes or until potatoes are fork-tender. Drain. Let potatoes cool.

2. Cook bacon in medium skillet over medium heat until crisp. Remove with slotted spoon. Crumble into large bowl; set aside. Drain all but 3 tablespoons drippings from skillet.

3. For dressing, cook and stir onion in skillet until tender. Remove from heat. Combine vinegar, water, sugar, salt, mustard seeds and prepared mustard in skillet. Keep warm.

4. Peel potatoes and cut into ¼-inch slices. Add potatoes to bowl with bacon. Pour warm dressing over potato mixture; toss to coat evenly. Top with parsley and sprinkle with paprika. Serve hot or cold.

Makes 6 to 8 servings

traditional german potato salad

thick potato chips with beer ketchup

Beer Ketchup (recipe follows)
1 quart peanut oil
3 baking potatoes, scrubbed
Sea salt and black pepper

1. Prepare Beer Ketchup. Heat oil in deep pan (oil should come up sides at least 3 inches) to 345°F.

2. Slice potatoes into ¼-inch-thick slices. Lower into oil in batches. Fry 2 to 3 minutes per side, flipping to brown evenly on both sides. Drain on paper towels and immediately sprinkle with salt and pepper.

3. Serve with Beer Ketchup.

Makes 4 servings

beer ketchup

¾ cup ketchup
¼ cup beer
1 tablespoon Worcestershire sauce
¼ teaspoon onion powder
Ground red pepper

Mix all ingredients in small saucepan. Bring to a boil. Reduce heat; simmer 2 to 3 minutes. Remove from heat and let cool. Cover and store in refrigerator until ready to use.

Makes about 1 cup ketchup

tater tip

If the potatoes begin browning too quickly, turn down the heat and wait for the oil to cool to the proper temperature. Too high a temperature will not cook the potatoes completely, and too low a temperature will make the chips soggy.

thick potato chips with beer ketchup

grilled potato salad

Dressing

- **4 tablespoons country-style Dijon mustard**
- **1 tablespoon white wine or apple cider vinegar**
- **3 tablespoons olive oil**
- **2 tablespoons chopped fresh dill**
- **½ teaspoon salt**
- **¼ teaspoon black pepper**

Salad

- **2 pounds small red potatoes**
- **2 tablespoons olive oil**
- **1 green onion, thinly sliced**

1. Combine all dressing ingredients in glass measuring cup; stir well. Set aside.

2. Bring large saucepan salted water to a boil over medium-high heat. Cut potatoes into ½-inch slices. Add potatoes to water; boil about 5 minutes. Drain; return potatoes to saucepan. Drizzle with 2 tablespoons oil; toss lightly.

3. Prepare grill for direct cooking. Spray 1 side of large sheet of foil with nonstick cooking spray. Transfer potatoes to foil; fold into packet. Place potato packet on grid over medium-high heat. Grill 10 minutes or until potatoes are tender. Transfer potatoes to serving bowl. Sprinkle with green onion. Toss gently with reserved dressing. Serve warm.

Makes 4 servings

grilled potato salad

tuna niçoise salad

1 cup WISH-BONE® Italian Dressing,* divided
1 pound tuna or salmon steaks or 2 cans (6 ounces each) tuna, drained and flaked
12 ounces potatoes, unpeeled and cubed (about 2½ cups)
8 ounces green beans, trimmed and halved (about 2½ cups)
8 cups mesclun or mixed salad greens
2 hard-cooked eggs, cut into wedges
1 medium tomato, cut into wedges
½ cup pitted kalamata or ripe olives, halved

**Also terrific with WISH-BONE® Robusto Italian Dressing.*

Pour ¼ cup WISH-BONE® Italian Dressing over tuna in large, shallow nonaluminum baking dish or resealable plastic bag; turn to coat. Cover, or close bag, and marinate in refrigerator 30 minutes.

Cover potatoes with water in 2-quart saucepan; bring to a boil over high heat. Reduce heat to low and simmer 5 minutes. Add green beans and continue cooking an additional 5 minutes or until potatoes are tender and green beans are crisp-tender; drain. Toss warm potatoes and green beans with ¼ cup Dressing.

Remove tuna from marinade, discarding marinade. Grill or broil tuna, turning once and brushing frequently with ¼ cup Dressing, 8 minutes or until tuna is desired doneness. Cut tuna into thin slices.

Arrange salad greens on serving platter. Top with potato and green bean mixture, eggs, tomato, sliced tuna and olives. Drizzle with remaining Dressing.

Makes 6 servings

Prep Time: 20 minutes
Marinate Time: 30 minutes
Cook Time: 20 minutes

tuna niçoise salad

vegetable potato salad

1 envelope LIPTON® RECIPE SECRETS® Vegetable Soup Mix
1 cup HELLMANN'S® or BEST FOODS® Real Mayonnaise
2 teaspoons white vinegar
2 pounds red or all-purpose potatoes, cooked and cut into chunks
¼ cup finely chopped red onion (optional)

1. In large bowl, combine soup mix, mayonnaise and vinegar.
2. Add potatoes and onion; toss well. Chill 2 hours. **Makes 6 servings**

Prep Time: 20 minutes
Chill Time: 2 hours

herbed potato chips

Olive oil cooking spray
2 medium red potatoes (about 8 ounces)
1 tablespoon olive oil
2 tablespoons minced fresh dill, thyme or rosemary leaves *or* 2 teaspoons dried dill weed, thyme or rosemary
¼ teaspoon garlic salt
⅛ teaspoon black pepper
1¼ cups sour cream

1. Preheat oven to 450°F. Spray baking sheets with cooking spray.
2. Cut potatoes crosswise into very thin slices, about 1/16 inch thick. Pat dry with paper towels. Arrange potato slices in single layer on prepared baking sheets; coat potatoes with cooking spray.
3. Bake 10 minutes; turn slices over. Brush with oil. Combine dill, garlic salt and pepper in small bowl; sprinkle evenly onto potato slices. Continue baking 5 to 10 minutes or until potatoes are golden brown. Cool on baking sheets. Serve with sour cream. **Makes 6 servings**

potato and blue cheese salad

1 pound new or fingerling potatoes
½ teaspoon salt
½ cup shredded radicchio
¼ cup pitted, halved kalamata or niçoise olives
¼ cup (1 ounce) crumbled Gorgonzola cheese
2½ tablespoons olive oil
1 teaspoon white wine vinegar
1 teaspoon Dijon mustard
¼ teaspoon black pepper

1. Place potatoes and salt in medium saucepan; add water to cover. Bring to a boil; cook about 20 to 25 minutes or until potatoes are tender. Drain well; cut into bite-size pieces.

2. Combine potatoes, radicchio, olives and cheese in large bowl. Whisk oil, vinegar, mustard and pepper in small bowl. Pour over potato mixture; stir gently to coat. Let stand 30 minutes for flavors to blend. Serve at room temperature. **Makes 4 to 6 servings**

Variation: Replace Gorgonzola cheese with feta cheese, and use sun-dried tomatoes and fresh basil instead of radicchio.

mini new potato bites

1½ pounds new potatoes (about 15 potatoes)
4 ounces (½ of 8-ounce package) PHILADELPHIA® Cream Cheese, softened
2 tablespoons BREAKSTONE'S® or KNUDSEN® Sour Cream
2 tablespoons KRAFT® 100% Grated Parmesan Cheese
4 slices OSCAR MAYER® Bacon, cooked, crumbled
2 tablespoons snipped fresh chives

PLACE potatoes in large saucepan; add enough water to cover. Bring to boil. Reduce heat to medium-low; cook 15 minutes or until potatoes are tender.

MIX cream cheese, sour cream and Parmesan cheese; cover. Refrigerate until ready to use.

DRAIN potatoes. Cool slightly. Cut potatoes in half; cut small piece from bottom of each potato half so potato lies flat. Place on serving platter. Top each potato half with 1 teaspoon of the cream cheese mixture. Sprinkle with bacon and chives.

Makes 15 servings, 2 topped potato halves each

Make Ahead: These potatoes are delicious served hot or cold.

Substitution: Substitute PHILADELPHIA® Chive & Onion Cream Cheese Spread for the regular cream cheese for added flavor.

Prep Time: 30 minutes

mini new potato bites

creamy red potato salad

3 pounds red bliss or new potatoes, cut into ¾-inch chunks
½ cup WISH-BONE® Italian Dressing*
¾ cup HELLMANN'S® or BEST FOODS® Real Mayonnaise
½ cup sliced green onions
1 teaspoon Dijon mustard
1 teaspoon lemon juice
⅛ teaspoon ground black pepper

**Also terrific with WISH-BONE® Robusto Italian or House Italian Dressing.*

Cover potatoes with water in 4-quart saucepot; bring to a boil over medium-high heat. Reduce heat to low and simmer 10 minutes or until potatoes are tender. Drain and cool slightly.

Combine all ingredients except potatoes in large salad bowl. Add potatoes and toss gently. Serve chilled or at room temperature.

Makes 10 servings

Prep Time: 15 minutes
Cook Time: 10 minutes

New potatoes are young potatoes. They may be any variety, but most often are round reds. New potatoes can be as small as marbles or almost as large as full-size potatoes, and they should have a very thin wispy skin. The sugar in these young potatoes has not completely converted to starch, so they have a crisp, waxy texture. They are excellent in potato salads, such as this one, as well as roasted alone or with other vegetables.

sweet potato & fruit salad

2 sweet potatoes (about 1¼ pounds)
1 unpeeled small Granny Smith apple, chopped
¼ cup chopped celery
1 container (6 ounces) plain yogurt
2 tablespoons orange juice
½ to 1 teaspoon grated fresh ginger
½ teaspoon curry powder
⅛ teaspoon salt
½ cup cinnamon-coated nuts, divided
¼ cup drained mandarin oranges

1. Pierce sweet potatoes in several places with fork and place on microwavable dish. Cover loosely with microwave-safe plastic wrap. Microwave on HIGH 6 to 7 minutes, turning over halfway through cooking time. Cool completely.

2. Peel potatoes and cut into 1-inch pieces. Combine potatoes, apple and celery in large bowl.

3. Combine yogurt, orange juice, ginger, curry powder and salt in small bowl. Add to potato mixture; mix well. Add half of nuts; stir gently. Top with remaining nuts and oranges. Refrigerate until ready to serve.

Makes 4 to 6 servings

Variations: Use your favorite type of roasted nut. Add some chopped jalapeño pepper for a spicy version.

sweet potato & fruit salad

garden potato salad with basil-yogurt dressing

6 new potatoes, quartered
8 ounces asparagus, cut into 1-inch pieces
1¼ cups red, yellow or green bell pepper strips
⅔ cup plain yogurt
¼ cup sliced green onions
2 tablespoons chopped pitted black olives
1½ tablespoons chopped fresh basil *or* 1½ teaspoons dried basil
1 tablespoon chopped fresh thyme *or* 1 teaspoon dried thyme
1 tablespoon white vinegar
2 teaspoons sugar
Dash ground red pepper

1. Bring 3 cups water to a boil in large saucepan over high heat. Add potatoes; return to a boil. Reduce heat to medium-low. Simmer, covered, 8 minutes.

2. Add asparagus and bell peppers; return to a boil over high heat. Reduce heat to medium-low. Simmer, covered, about 3 minutes or until potatoes are just tender and asparagus and bell peppers are crisp-tender. Drain.

3. Meanwhile, combine yogurt, green onions, olives, basil, thyme, vinegar, sugar and ground red pepper in large bowl. Add vegetables; toss to combine. Refrigerate, covered, until well chilled.

Makes 4 servings

acknowledgments

The publisher would like to thank the companies and organizations listed below for the use of their recipes and photographs in this publication.

Campbell Soup Company

Dole Food Company, Inc.

Kraft Foods Global, Inc.

Michael Foods, Inc.

Mrs. Dash® SALT-FREE SEASONING BLENDS

Nestlé USA

Ortega®, A Division of B&G Foods, Inc.

Reckitt Benckiser Inc.

Tyson Foods, Inc.

Unilever

A

Apples: Sweet Potato & Fruit Salad, 136
Asparagus: Garden Potato Salad with Basil-Yogurt Dressing, 138

B

Bacon
- Bacon and Cheese Brunch Potatoes, 94
- Bacon Onion Cornish Hens with Potatoes, 34
- Easy Cheesy Potatoes, 108
- Mini New Potato Bites, 132
- Picnic Potato Salad, 118
- Roasted Red Potato Bites, 116
- Swiss Onion Potatoes Rosti, 58
- Traditional German Potato Salad, 122
- Two-Toned Stuffed Potatoes, 110

Bacon and Cheese Brunch Potatoes, 94
Bacon Onion Cornish Hens with Potatoes, 34
Baked Sweet Potato Fries with Spicy Apricot Dipping Sauce, 76
Beans, Canned: Hearty Vegetable Stew, 6
Beef
- Hearty Beef and Potato Casserole, 38
- Italian-Style Shepherd's Pie, 32
- Potato Taco Lasagna, 40
- Rainbow Casserole, 42
- Skillet Steak & Potatoes, 44
- Taco-Topped Potatoes, 98
- Yankee Pot Roast and Vegetables, 26

Beer Ketchup, 124
Blue Cheese
- Blue Cheese Potato Soup with Olive Tapenade, 18
- Potato and Blue Cheese Salad, 131
- Two-Cheese Potato and Cauliflower Soup, 20

Blue Cheese Potato Soup with Olive Tapenade, 18
Bratwurst Skillet Breakfast, 35

C

Cabbage
- Bratwurst Skillet Breakfast, 35
- Cabbage Colcannon, 50
- Hearty Vegetable Stew, 6
- Peasant Potatoes, 83

Cabbage Colcannon, 50
Carrots
- Curried Carrot and Potato Soup, 8
- Hearty Vegetable Stew, 6
- Oven-Roasted Root Vegetables, 102
- Portuguese Potato & Greens Soup, 68
- Potato Cheddar Soup, 4
- Vegetable Casserole, 88
- Yankee Pot Roast and Vegetables, 26

Casseroles
- Chili Meatloaf and Potato Bake, 28
- Easy Cheesy Potatoes, 108
- Gratin of Two Potatoes, 104
- Ham, Poblano and Potato Casserole, 46
- Hearty Beef and Potato Casserole, 38
- Italian-Style Shepherd's Pie, 32
- Mexican Hash Brown Bake, 102
- Potato, Beer and Cheese Gratin, 114
- Potato Taco Lasagna, 40
- Rainbow Casserole, 42
- Scalloped Potato-Onion Bake, 112
- Vegetable Casserole, 88

Cauliflower
- Cauliflower and Potato Masala, 64
- Creamy Cauliflower Bisque, 14
- Potato-Cauliflower Mash, 86
- Two-Cheese Potato and Cauliflower Soup, 20

Cauliflower and Potato Masala, 64
Chicken (*see also* **Cornish Hens**)
- Chile Verde Chicken Stew, 22
- Spanish Tortilla, 70

Chickpeas: Spicy African Chickpea and Sweet Potato Stew, 60
Chile Pepper & Corn Cream Chowder, 16
Chile Verde Chicken Stew, 22
Chili Meatloaf and Potato Bake, 28
Chipotle Lamb Chops with Crispy Potatoes, 36
Chive & Onion Mashed Potatoes, 82
Chorizo and Papa Burritos, 66
Chunky Ranch Potatoes, 92
Corn
Chile Pepper & Corn Cream Chowder, 16
Cream-Cheesy Garden Chowder, 10
Ham, Poblano and Potato Casserole, 46
Italian-Style Shepherd's Pie, 32
Skillet Steak & Potatoes, 44
Cornish Hens: Bacon Onion Cornish Hens with Potatoes, 34
Cream Cheese
Chile Pepper & Corn Cream Chowder, 16
Chive & Onion Mashed Potatoes, 82
Cream-Cheesy Garden Chowder, 10
Mini New Potato Bites, 132
Cream-Cheesy Garden Chowder, 10
Creamy Cauliflower Bisque, 14
Creamy Golden Mushroom Mashed Potatoes, 74
Creamy Red Potato Salad, 134
Creamy Smashed Red Potatoes with Cheese, 78
Curried Carrot and Potato Soup, 8

E

Easy Cheesy Potatoes, 108

F

Fish & Chips, 54

G

Garden Potato Salad with Basil-Yogurt Dressing, 138
Garlic Fries, 92
German Potato Salad with Grilled Sausage, 48
Gnocchi: Potato Gnocchi with Tomato Sauce, 62
Gratin of Two Potatoes, 104
Green Beans
Rustic Vegetable Soup, 6
Tuna Niçoise Salad, 128
Vegetable Casserole, 88
Grilled Potato Salad, 126
Grilling Recipes
Bacon Onion Cornish Hens with Potatoes, 34
German Potato Salad with Grilled Sausage, 48
Grilled Potato Salad, 126
Tuna Niçoise Salad, 128

H

Ham
Ham and Sweet Potato Skillet, 30
Ham, Poblano and Potato Casserole, 46
Ham and Sweet Potato Skillet, 30
Ham, Poblano and Potato Casserole, 46
Hearty Beef and Potato Casserole, 38
Hearty Vegetable Stew, 6
Herbed Potato Chips, 130

I

Italian-Style Shepherd's Pie, 32

L

Lamb: Chipotle Lamb Chops with Crispy Potatoes, 36
Lemon-Mint Potatoes, 80

M

Mediterranean-Style Roasted Vegetables, 106
Mexican Hash Brown Bake, 102
Mini New Potato Bites, 132

N

New Potatoes and Peas, 86

O

Olives
Blue Cheese Potato Soup with Olive Tapenade, 18
Tuna Niçoise Salad, 128
Oven-Roasted Root Vegetables, 102

P

Parmesan Potato Wedges, 78
Pasta: Pasta & Potatoes with Pesto, 50
Pasta & Potatoes with Pesto, 50
Peas
New Potatoes and Peas, 86
Pasta & Potatoes with Pesto, 50
Rainbow Casserole, 42
Peasant Potatoes, 83
Peppery Potato Soup, 24
Picnic Potato Salad, 118
Portuguese Potato & Greens Soup, 68
Potato and Blue Cheese Salad, 131
Potato & Spinach Soup with Gouda, 15
Potato, Beer and Cheese Gratin, 114
Potato-Cauliflower Mash, 86
Potato Cheddar Soup, 4
Potato Chips
Herbed Potato Chips, 130
Thick Potato Chips with Beer Ketchup, 124
Potato Gnocchi with Tomato Sauce, 62
Potato Pierogi, 56
Potato Soup with Arugula, 12
Potato Taco Lasagna, 40

R

Rainbow Casserole, 42
Roasted Peppers and Potatoes, 84
Roasted Red Potato Bites, 116
Rustic Vegetable Soup, 6

S

Salads
Creamy Red Potato Salad, 134
Garden Potato Salad with Basil-Yogurt Dressing, 138
German Potato Salad with Grilled Sausage, 48
Grilled Potato Salad, 126
Picnic Potato Salad, 118
Potato and Blue Cheese Salad, 131
Sweet Potato & Fruit Salad, 136
Traditional German Potato Salad, 122
Tuna Niçoise Salad, 128
Vegetable Potato Salad, 130
Salsa
Chili Meatloaf and Potato Bake, 28
Mexican Hash Brown Bake, 102
Potato Taco Lasagna, 40
Sausage
Bratwurst Skillet Breakfast, 35
Chorizo and Papa Burritos, 66
German Potato Salad with Grilled Sausage, 48
Peasant Potatoes, 83
Portuguese Potato & Greens Soup, 68
Savory Herb Roasted Potatoes, 103
Scalloped Potato-Onion Bake, 112
Seafood
Fish & Chips, 54
Tuna Niçoise Salad, 128
Skillet Steak & Potatoes, 44
Slow Cooker Recipes
Bacon and Cheese Brunch Potatoes, 94
Chunky Ranch Potatoes, 92
Creamy Cauliflower Bisque, 14
Lemon-Mint Potatoes, 80
Parmesan Potato Wedges, 78

Slow Cooker Recipes *(continued)*
Peasant Potatoes, 83
Peppery Potato Soup, 24
Potato & Spinach Soup with Gouda, 15
Potato Cheddar Soup, 4
Rustic Vegetable Soup, 6
Yankee Pot Roast and Vegetables, 26
Soup, Canned
Creamy Golden Mushroom Mashed Potatoes, 74
New Potatoes and Peas, 86
Scalloped Potato-Onion Bake, 112
Soups & Stews, 4–25
Portuguese Potato & Greens Soup, 68
Spicy African Chickpea and Sweet Potato Stew, 60
Spanish Tapas Potatoes (Patatas Bravas), 52
Spanish Tortilla, 70
Spice Paste, 60
Spicy African Chickpea and Sweet Potato Stew, 60
Spicy Apricot Dipping Sauce, 76
Spicy Steak Fries, 72
Spinach
Potato & Spinach Soup with Gouda, 15
Potato Taco Lasagna, 40
Vegetable Casserole, 88
Squash
Italian-Style Shepherd's Pie, 32
Spanish Tortilla, 70
Sweet Potatoes
Baked Sweet Potato Fries with Spicy Apricot Dipping Sauce, 76
Gratin of Two Potatoes, 104
Ham and Sweet Potato Skillet, 30
Spicy African Chickpea and Sweet Potato Stew, 60
Sweet Potato & Fruit Salad, 136
Thyme-Scented Roasted Sweet Potatoes and Onions, 100
Two-Toned Stuffed Potatoes, 110
Swiss Onion Potatoes Rosti, 58
Swiss-Style Twice Baked Potatoes, 96

T

Taco-Topped Potatoes, 98
Tex-Mex Potato Skins, 120
Thick Potato Chips with Beer Ketchup, 124
Thyme-Scented Roasted Sweet Potatoes and Onions, 100
Tomatoes, Fresh
Cauliflower and Potato Masala, 64
Skillet Steak & Potatoes, 44
Taco-Topped Potatoes, 98
Tomato Sauce, 63
Tuna Niçoise Salad, 128
Tomato Sauce, 63
Tortillas
Chorizo and Papa Burritos, 66
Spanish Tortilla, 70
Traditional German Potato Salad, 122
Tuna Niçoise Salad, 128
Turkey: Chili Meatloaf and Potato Bake, 28
Two-Cheese Potato and Cauliflower Soup, 20
Two-Toned Stuffed Potatoes, 110

V

Vegetable Casserole, 88
Vegetable Potato Salad, 130
Vegetables, Mixed: Rustic Vegetable Soup, 6

Y

Yankee Pot Roast and Vegetables, 26
Yellow Couscous, 62

Z

Zestup Ketchup, 90
Zippy Oven Fries, 90

metric conversion chart

VOLUME MEASUREMENTS (dry)

1/8 teaspoon = 0.5 mL
1/4 teaspoon = 1 mL
1/2 teaspoon = 2 mL
3/4 teaspoon = 4 mL
1 teaspoon = 5 mL
1 tablespoon = 15 mL
2 tablespoons = 30 mL
1/4 cup = 60 mL
1/3 cup = 75 mL
1/2 cup = 125 mL
2/3 cup = 150 mL
3/4 cup = 175 mL
1 cup = 250 mL
2 cups = 1 pint = 500 mL
3 cups = 750 mL
4 cups = 1 quart = 1 L

VOLUME MEASUREMENTS (fluid)

1 fluid ounce (2 tablespoons) = 30 mL
4 fluid ounces (1/2 cup) = 125 mL
8 fluid ounces (1 cup) = 250 mL
12 fluid ounces (1 1/2 cups) = 375 mL
16 fluid ounces (2 cups) = 500 mL

WEIGHTS (mass)

1/2 ounce = 15 g
1 ounce = 30 g
3 ounces = 90 g
4 ounces = 120 g
8 ounces = 225 g
10 ounces = 285 g
12 ounces = 360 g
16 ounces = 1 pound = 450 g

DIMENSIONS

1/16 inch = 2 mm
1/8 inch = 3 mm
1/4 inch = 6 mm
1/2 inch = 1.5 cm
3/4 inch = 2 cm
1 inch = 2.5 cm

OVEN TEMPERATURES

250°F = 120°C
275°F = 140°C
300°F = 150°C
325°F = 160°C
350°F = 180°C
375°F = 190°C
400°F = 200°C
425°F = 220°C
450°F = 230°C

BAKING PAN SIZES

Utensil	Size in Inches/Quarts	Metric Volume	Size in Centimeters
Baking or Cake Pan (square or rectangular)	8×8×2	2 L	20×20×5
	9×9×2	2.5 L	23×23×5
	12×8×2	3 L	30×20×5
	13×9×2	3.5 L	33×23×5
Loaf Pan	8×4×3	1.5 L	20×10×7
	9×5×3	2 L	23×13×7
Round Layer Cake Pan	8×1½	1.2 L	20×4
	9×1½	1.5 L	23×4
Pie Plate	8×1¼	750 mL	20×3
	9×1¼	1 L	23×3
Baking Dish or Casserole	1 quart	1 L	—
	1½ quart	1.5 L	—
	2 quart	2 L	—